THE LEGAL RESEARCH SURVIVAL MANUAL

WITH VIDEO MODULES

Second Edition

Robert C. Berring

Professor of Law
Berkeley Law
University of California, Berkeley

Michael Levy

Associate Director, Berkeley Law Library
University of California, Berkeley

WEST
ACADEMIC
PUBLISHING

© 2002 Thomson West
© 2017 LEG, Inc. d/b/a West Academic
    444 Cedar Street, Suite 700
    St. Paul, MN 55101
    1-877-888-1330

ISBN: 978-1-68328-465-9

A NOTE ON SEX, DRUGS AND ROCK 'N' ROLL

No one reads the Introduction to books so we called this section "Sex, Drugs and Rock 'n' Roll" in the hopes that you actually will look at it. If you have made it this far, please read on, good karma awaits. There are a few things that you should know about this book.

First, this book is not intended as a comprehensive treatment of legal research. Other books fill that need. Our favorite is Kent Olson's Principles of Legal Research. It is a carefully written treatment of legal research. This means that it is fairly long and detailed. You know, the kind of thing that is good for you.

This book is different. In fact the book is only part of the package. Joined by Professors Lindsay Saffouri and Patricia Hurley of the Berkeley faculty, we have made a set of videos to go with the book. The videos are short and simple. They will not contain all of the detail of this book, but they provide the basics. Our mission is to supply you with the crucial information about legal research. We feel strongly that knowing the information in this book matters! If we could go door to door explaining it, we would. Making the videos seemed more practical.

Since you are holding the book right now, let's talk about it. It is written as a survival manual for first year law students. Our goal is to tell you what you need to know to get through the first year of law school, specifically the first semester. Maybe you will learn enough to help you get that first legal job. This does not mean that we think you should limit yourself to survival skills. We think that you should take a full-blown course in legal research. The reality is that very few law schools have the luxury of offering a complete course in legal research to first year students. Usually legal research is combined with legal writing and analysis. Frequently it is crammed into a few weeks. You can feel as if you have been thrown into the deep end of the pool and are expected to start swimming through sheer terror. This book is designed to help folks in such situations. If we had our way, each person who reads this book (and if we really had our way that would be zillions of people), will go on to take a course in Advanced Legal Research. Such a course would examine legal information in an analytical framework. We think that a full-fledged run at legal research can be exciting and challenging. But we are realists. Just because we think legal research is cool does not mean that you will find it to be so. This book is designed to get you through the night.

As you may have already noticed, we will adopt an informal style in presenting this information. We happen to think that legal research is a vitally interesting topic, but then we also believe that tapioca is delicious, so we know better than to trust our instincts. We decided that if we are going to give you the nuts and bolts of legal research, we will do it our own way. The book is filled with opinions and short cuts. Things that we think you are unlikely to have to deal with during your first year are missing altogether. We have tried to keep the tone light. Let's face it, we are both smart mouths from birth. We have also tried to keep it short. Remember, there are lots of places to go for more details. Our motto has been that less is more. The videos take this all one step further. No matter how you learn best, we try to get at you. Remember, if this does not work, we will show up at your door.

Since we are going to be informal, introductions are in order. Bob Berring is a professor of law at Berkeley Law School. He has been teaching courses in legal research and advanced legal research for, well, let's just say a long time. He also teaches Contracts, a fact which will intrude into the text at several points. (Bob also teaches courses about China, but that may not come up.) Michael Levy is a Lecturer and the Associate Librarian at Berkeley Law School. He has helped thousands of first year law students weather the first semester of law school, and unlike Bob he learned his skills at a time when computers were the center of the research enterprise. Michael is far better at web surfing than Bob. He also has a very fine British accent— check out the videos and enjoy for yourself.

If you are the kind of person who will only listen to information instead of reading it, or watching a video, return this book and procure the *Sum and Substance* audio series on Legal Research. As we just stated, we will try anything to reach you.

This book is being written in November of 2016. Everything we write here is true as of that date but this is a field where everything changes. When using any legal resource be sure and check the date on which it was published.

With that behind us, we can proceed. If you understand legal information it will make everything else in law school easier. It is the one skill that you will learn in law school that will have immediate application in the workplace. As the world of legal information shifts from paper to digital materials and as the legal marketplace becomes more and more cost conscious, good research skills will be valuable. We want to make you a better, smarter researcher. Let's see if we can do it.

OUR THANKS

We want to thank Elizabeth Edinger, Associate Clinical Professor and Director of the Law Library at Catholic University, co-author of the first edition of this text. Her influence remains. We would also like to thank Alex Williamson ('18) of the Berkeley Law School for her help in keeping the text in check and the screen grabs clear. Roxanne Livingston helped preparing the manuscript. Many useful suggestions from instructors of legal research and writing came to us via a survey conducted by West Academic, they helped us in shaping this book and the accompanying videos. As always, Bob thanks Leslie Berring for her help and inspiration.

Michael wants to thank his colleagues Kathleen Vanden Heuvel, Director, Berkeley Law Library and Marci Hoffman, Associate Director, Berkeley Law Library for their always sage advice and ongoing commitment to the enterprise of legal research. A final thanks to Michelle Quinn, Nico Quinn and Natalia Levy for keeping it all in perspective.

SUMMARY OF CONTENTS

TABLE OF CONTENTS

THE LEGAL RESEARCH SURVIVAL MANUAL

WITH VIDEO MODULES

Second Edition

CHAPTER 1

THINGS THAT YOU WILL ENCOUNTER IN YOUR FIRST SEMESTER

In this Chapter we will spend the bulk of our time discussing the avalanche of new forms of information that you will encounter in the first semester of law school. We will end with a bit of advice on how to survive the semester in one piece.

As a first year law student you will encounter a dizzying array of new sorts of materials. Some will be in paper, some will be computerized databases. Some will be websites and blogs. Some will be unique to legal education, others will be variants of tools that you have used before. Let's look at them one by one. We have sorted them into three categories:

- Things that you might actually purchase.
- The online services that will appear to be free.
- Resources that everyone will mention without explaining.

I. THINGS THAT YOU MIGHT BUY

a. Casebooks

At most law schools the first year is oddly reminiscent of high school. You have to take a set of assigned courses, you sit in assigned seats and you will get a locker for your books. You will need that locker. First year courses are invariably taught using "casebooks." Casebooks are huge, dinosaur-sized things that frequently run well over a thousand pages and weigh a ton. Here is perhaps the best advice that we will give you in this book: get the spine cut off your casebooks at a local copy shop, punch holes in the pages and put the book in a binder or two. That way you can work with the pages you need without giving yourself a hernia from hauling around eighty pounds of books. (Think we're joking? You'll see.) Some law school book stores now rent casebooks. This might be a path you want to take, though it is hard to restrain yourself from marking up the text.

The idea of the casebook sprang from the bearded head of Dean Christopher Columbus Langdell of the Harvard Law School. In 1870 Langdell created the modern form of the American law school at Harvard. There were other ways to get a legal education back then, and Langdell's ideas took decades to become dominant. But dominate they did. Legions of Harvard-trained law professors spread the doctrine and the model has replicated itself everywhere. Being a man of his time, Langdell thought that law was a science that was built on immutable principles. These scientific principles were to be found in cases. Langdell believed that if you read enough cases, and if those cases were arranged in the right order by wise professors, transcendent legal principles would emerge and the reader would thus be enlightened. For this reason the first casebooks contained only cases. That's right, only cases—nothing added to help the poor students.

No one believes that law is a science founded upon immutable principles anymore, but the device of learning law by reading cases remains firmly entrenched. Of course, modern casebooks do not contain only cases. Your casebook may contain bits of law review articles, parts of statutes, questions to ponder and explanatory commentary by the authors. Casebooks are frequently authored by teams of professors, and each may draw on his or her teaching experience in putting the book together. There has been a great deal of talk about abandoning the jumbo-sized printed casebook for some electronic format, but things have been slow to change. If you have not yet figured it out, law is a very conservative field. Some casebooks now have digital components that allow the reader access to an online version of the book and thus to work online on whatever device she might choose. There is a great deal of potential in these tools and they will be developing as you use them. But the printed casebook still holds sway in 2016. And most of the alternatives that have appeared to this point are more a matter of putting the casebook online, not a true revolution in how the information is presented.

Despite the changes since Langdell's time, the heart of the casebook is still the text of the judicial decision. They are, after all, called casebooks. Strangely though, it is rare that you will be given a complete decision to read. It is much more likely that the casebook will contain an excerpt of the opinion. Part of the art of producing a good casebook is being able to cut up the cases in ways that tease the law student (that's you) into seeing a point. The casebook may print only a page or two of a very long opinion. Most of the citations within the decision will be removed. Dissents will almost never be included. You will not be given the whole picture. The fact is that you will only be getting tiny peeks at the actual opinion. And you may be getting peeks at parts of an opinion that are outmoded, discredited or just wrong. The casebook may not tell you this; it may leave it up to you to work it out on your own. Many first year casebooks hide the ball. The authors of the casebook, and your professor, do not just tell you what the law is; instead they want you to puzzle it out. Just so you know, most casebooks come with a teacher's manual that explains to your professor what the casebook authors were trying to do. It hardly seems fair.

In the second and third year of law school you will take courses that are subject specific and focused. In the first year you take big common law courses that do not address any specific area at all. This is why the way one professor teaches Property can be completely different from the way another professor teaches it. Contracts, Torts, Criminal Law, Civil Procedure and Property were all being taught in the first year at Langdell's Harvard Law School in 1870. They still are being taught in most law schools. What does that tell you? It tells you that first year courses are really about teaching you to think and analyze. The casebook is designed to prod your thinking, not tell you what the law is. Not understanding this key point can lead to many long, frustrating nights for students who think that there must be a rational way to put the casebook's pieces together.

Based on the dire situation that we have described, you might think that there is little we can tell you about casebooks that can help you, but you should never underestimate us. One of the videos waxes at length on this topic. Here is our list of tips on using casebooks:

1. ***If you read a case in a casebook and have trouble
figuring it out, you can always go read the full text.*** Go to
Westlaw or Lexis (the two largest and most prominent online
legal research systems) and look it up. Bloomberg Law can also
perform this function for you, but that system has yet to take
root in most law schools. We will stick to Westlaw and Lexis
which are omnipresent in most of the discussion that follows. Or
take a real walk on the wild side and go pull the relevant case
reporter volume off the shelf in the law library. When you read
the version of the case as used by lawyers you will not only find
the full text of the decision but you will also find a variety of
features designed to explain what is going on. (We will talk about
these features in Chapter 2.) The publishers of judicial decisions
for lawyers design them to make things as easy for the
practitioner as possible. You will be told who the parties are, who
won, and why. Since the casebook often is designed to confuse
and amaze you, a research tool that is at least ***trying*** to make
the law clear is a godsend.

A spate of web-based services will offer summaries of the
opinions that you find in your casebook. Some are free, some
offered by subscription. In the fall of 2016 a service titled
Quimbee was popular, but such things change quickly. Such
services provide a summary of the case, perhaps with guidance
on how the case fits into the law. Here is an area where it is
CRUCIAL to check the source of the information. Is it an
established provider or is it produced by a disgruntled second
year law student in his attic? They can be a help but taking a
look at the case in the form that a practicing lawyer would see it
remains the best back-up.

2. ***The casebook is carefully organized to make
certain points.*** Frequently folks plunge into the casebooks,
madly briefing each case, never seeing the forest for the trees. It
really helps to understand where the casebook authors think
that they are taking you. Instead of reading your assignment in
the casebook in isolation, look at the Table of Contents of the
book. Most casebooks have a very detailed Table of Contents so
that you can see how the authors break down the subject. Check
how the authors have organized the book and look at the
subdivisions. You should try to psych out what the authors are

trying to accomplish. Bob always tells his Contracts students that when they read a case they should try and figure out why the case is there. What purpose does it serve? One of the things that we will repeat over and over in this book is "context." Put what you are reading into the context of the book.

3. ***Casebooks are little artificial worlds, where you are told only what the author wants you to know, in the way that the author wants you to know it.*** Escaping that universe is often a good idea. Everything that follows in this chapter offers one form of escape or another. Mastering the labyrinthine structure of one of the notoriously tough casebooks may, in theory, build strong minds and resilient reasoning, (heaven knows that Professor Langdell would approve), but when nothing makes sense and the rest of the world is asleep, the average first year law student needs somewhere to go for help. Fair is fair. What follows are the most common places to go for that help. They will be treated in order of seriousness.

b. Hornbooks

Because casebooks are incomplete at best and downright opaque at worst, students have needed help since Langdell's time. The first tool to develop as a way of helping the struggling law student was the "hornbook." A hornbook is book that explains a single area of the law in straightforward fashion. In a hornbook the authors try to set out the law, using narrative commentary. Instead of puzzling things out by reading a string of cases, you are simply given a textual description of what the law is. There is at least one hornbook for every major law school subject, and sometimes several. Hornbooks contain what is called "black letter law." Black letter law is an explanation of what the law is.

Because the law is unbelievably squishy and is always filled with exceptions, hornbooks are often very misleading. Remember that we live in a federal jurisdiction where there are fifty-one separate legal systems, and in any one jurisdiction it may be hard to determine what the law is. But hornbooks try. They represent solid attempts at explaining what the law is. To the desperate first year student, reeling from conflicting cases on a subject like unconscionable contracts, a hornbook will offer a bit of lucid explanation.

Like their gnarlier cousin the casebook, most hornbooks have a good Table of Contents. These Tables of Contents are done in great detail so that you can find just what you want. Hornbooks also have a Table of Cases. These allow you to see if a particular case that concerns you—perhaps one from your casebook—is discussed in the text and where to find it if it is. You will be surprised how often this happens. Many casebooks in a particular subject will use the same core of cases so the hornbooks discuss them, too. If you are baffled by the meaning of a case in your casebook, try looking it up in a hornbook.

When Bob graduated from law school hornbooks were still viewed as somehow unclean by most professors. Students were not supposed to need the help. Over the years they have grown larger and more complex. Some have become powerful persuasive authority, cited by even the Supreme Court of the United States. Not all of them have achieved that status, but the intellectual inflation has taken hold. This means that many hornbooks are now pretty complex. Rather than just explaining the law they may drift into an academic discussion that is about as easy to read as ancient Hittite texts. Thus you might find a hornbook discussion of your unconscionable contract question and you will still not understand it. Don't worry, there will be more help on the way.

One good thing about hornbooks is that they are usually available at your law library. Ask a librarian and they will point you towards the best ones.

c.   Nutshells

Nutshells are a paperback series put out by West Academic, a large publisher of legal materials. The idea of the *Nutshell* is simple: provide a straightforward, concise explanation of an area of law. Keep it easy to read, hold down the footnotes and just tell the reader what she needs to know. The *Nutshell* has no pretensions about being authoritative; it is just there to help. A *Nutshell* has a Table of Contents and a Case Table, but these are pretty primitive.

Will the *Nutshell* help you? Once again, you can give it a test drive before you buy one. Your law school library should have the *Nutshells*. There are *Nutshells* for each of the first year subjects, and some for subdivisions of those topics. Each runs a couple hundred pages in a pocket-sized volume. Check one out and find out if it works for you. The quality varies and one man's meat is another man's poison, so you never know. Some faculty think of *Nutshells* as being sort of sleazy, so don't quote them to your professor in the classroom. If you try quoting a *Nutshell* to your professor you might end up getting fed to the Socratic vegematic. Use *Nutshells* to inform yourself, get a handle on the issues, and get the context.

d.   Sum and Substance

West Academic also produces an audio series on a wide variety of legal topics. Among the titles there is one set to cover each first year topic. The recordings are made by professors who teach in the subject area. Why would you want audio? Some folks just learn better by listening, and if you are such a person this series may help you. If you have a long commute the *Sum and Substance* series might be a painless way to get some context. (Wearing headphones in class is a bad idea, however.) If all else fails, they may be a great way to get to sleep after a stressful day. Your law library may have the series, it is worth checking if you like to listen to your law.

e.   Outlines

Let's say that you cannot figure out what the professor is getting at. The casebook just confuses you. The canned case briefs that you find online are just pieces of the puzzle and the relevant hornbook only makes it worse. It is at this point that folks turn to "outlines." (Look, we know that some folks go to the outlines first, but we can all pretend, right?) Outlines are the underground of legal education. Everyone uses them. Trust me, everyone. The outline just, well, outlines what the law is. When you reach a point where all the bits and pieces of classroom discussion are rattling around in your brain until you feel that you might easily weep, the outline just lays it all out in a way that can easily be cried over. It may oversimplify, but it does give you the rules you need to know.

As a first year professor, Bob has opinions about outlines. He advises his students to use them, but beseeches them to wait until about half-way through the first semester. It really helps to mix it up in the classroom on your own for a while—see if the old case method magic works for you, and play the professor's game and try to learn to think like a lawyer. But when you reach the point where your brain is turning to tapioca and nothing is making sense, then go ahead and use the outline.

Which outline to use? Outlines come in many shapes and sizes. Folks have used the *Gilbert Law Summaries* series for years. Since the faculty who write the *Gilbert* titles sign their name, they have a little more heft. The *Emanuel Law Outlines* series is also well-established and has a stable of good authors. Westlaw also has free summaries of its *Black Letter Outline Series* online. (They are also in print). The very best outlines are the ones used in bar review courses, and sometimes you can get your hands on those. These are very fine because they are designed to convey great dollops of information in a lean, mean fashion. Sometimes there are local variants of outlines that are better than any standard national product could be. At many law schools student organizations keep outlines of first year courses on file. If you join a club or group, they may have a bank of outlines keyed to your professor and your class just waiting for you. Be forewarned, however, these outlines are generally donated by past students, some of whom may have put exceptional care into their outlines, whereas others may have, well, not. Ask some second year students what outlines folks at your law school use.

Avoid the natural inclination to simply put the name of your case into the Google search box and find a case brief. Free summaries are out there. But they may be over-simplified or just wrong. The great question for the researcher in 2016 concerns authority. Who wrote that free summary? Why trust them? Life as a first year law student is hard enough. There is no reason to go to class armed only with a questionable summary of the case at hand.

Use the outline with care. Most first year law school professors are going to care more about how you think and reason than a list of rules. Still, the outlines can give you a structure on which to build your ideas.

It is worth noting that West Academic now provides electronic access to many of their study aids—outlines, nutshells and hornbooks. You should check with your law library to see if they subscribe to this product.

II. THE MIGHTY ONLINE SYSTEMS

There are two full-text online legal information systems that will be central elements in your legal education. A third is trying desperately to join the game. Westlaw and Lexis are great shimmering cyberspace libraries of legal information. (Bloomberg Law has built an impressive system itself, but it has not yet deeply penetrated into most law schools.) Each system contains the full text of judicial opinions, statutes, administrative rules and more related legal information than any three dimensional library could ever hope to house.[1] As a 21st Century law student you are a very lucky duck, because you will be given, yes given, access to these systems for free. In fact your law library is paying a large fee for your use of them, although even then the cost is deeply subsidized. Nor will you just be given access to these Rolls Royce systems in the law library. You will get home access, in-person training, a blizzard of manuals, crib sheets and even a 1-800 number to call for research help. Westlaw and Lexis are engaged in the equivalent of a duel to the death. They want you to love them so that when you leave law school you will want to use (and pay them full price for) their product. This makes life good for law students. The good folks at Bloomberg Law want your love too. But at this point Westlaw and Lexis have the boots on the ground at almost every law school.

We will discuss each system in this text. Michael will devote an entire video to describing them. The most important message that we can give you is: *TAKE THE TRAINING that the systems offer!!* The typical human learns only as much as he or she has to know to operate any system. As a species we loathe reading

---

[1]   In defense of three dimensional libraries, though, we must speak. The brick and mortar of your university law library will house more actual material than is contained in either Westlaw or Lexis. If you want to do academic, scholarly research, you could do much better than using only Lexis and/or Westlaw.

directions. Westlaw and Lexis are both designed with very snazzy front-ends that make them easy to use intuitively. Let's face it, a chimp could use these systems and get results. Do not limit yourself like that. Take the systems seriously. Ease of use does not automatically translate to quality of results. You can do better than that chimp. (We know you can!) Exploit the free training that these companies provide. Don't just accept the free t-shirts and visors, seek out the advanced training. Learn it now when it is free. Each of these systems has incredible power if you know how to use it. Do not be one of the chimps who only know how to put search terms in the box. Find out about the bells and whistles. Time invested now will be worth it. It is not hard to be a star.

The second message that we wish to convey is that these puppies are not just libraries of cases, or case finding tools. Westlaw and Lexis are full-blown universes of information. There is always more there than you think.

There are other online systems making headway. Some are driven by idealists who believe information should be free, others recognize that lawyers are a great source of lucre. Leaner systems pop up all the time. Systems like FastCase, Casemaker and FindLaw are representative of efforts to provide cheaper access to legal information. Ravel is a system being built using a different search approach. Michael will describe all this to you in a video. But it is unlikely that you will encounter these in your first year. Only the major players can afford the cost of sending trainers to every law school and offering so much to each law student. This could well change, but right now that is the world that you will find.

III. OTHER TOOLS THAT YOU WILL ENCOUNTER

Since every law school teaches pretty much the same set of courses to first year law students (you will be called 1Ls at most schools), we can predict a few of the other legal sources that you will run into during your first semester.

a. Dictionaries

An acquaintance of ours who is a successful lawyer contends that the first year of law school is really about learning vocabulary. We might not go that far, but it is important that you learn to use words with care. When you are reading a case, if there is a word that you do not understand, look it up in a legal dictionary. Some words, (e.g. "remittitur"), will stick out because they are new. Others, (e.g. "consideration"), will be familiar words, but they will have special meanings. The rule of thumb is that it is better to check. When reading cases you have to go word by word, line by line. Do not fake it; look it up.

Every law school law library will have a copy of ***Black's Law Dictionary***. The new edition by Bryan Garner is really well done and easy to use. But don't buy one unless you find that you will use it. Try it first. If you really want a portable dictionary that you can carry with you (something that is not a bad idea if you are as uninformed as we were when we arrived at law school), you might consider purchasing one of the paperback dictionaries. *Black's Law Dictionary* is a large and heavy and, although you will have pumped up your biceps lugging casebooks around, it may be too much for you. The smaller ones are not as authoritative, but they will often provide the help you need.

The law library will also have a copy of Garner's ***Modern Legal Usage***. This reference makes an effort to show you how the word is actually used, not just provide you with a definition. It gives you the context—there's that word again—of the language. When you are not sure about a phrase or how to write something, this can be a big help.

b. Citation Manuals

As you will learn in subsequent chapters, citing to your source with precision will be an important component of legal research. For many generations the Bible of legal citation has been ***The Uniform System of Citation***. It is almost always called by its nickname, ***The Bluebook***, because of the color of its cover. This guide is published by the law review staffs at Harvard, Yale, Columbia and Penn. It is a goldmine for these institutions, because almost every law student has to buy and use one. Those who join a law review staff at a law school must learn the intricacies of it. Indeed "to bluebook" became a verb, one that usually described a tedious and mournful process for law students. *The Bluebook* has always been idiosyncratic and hard to use. Forcing new students to master it has been a hazing ritual. (We should own up that one of us despises *The Bluebook*—could you tell?) A good citation guide should be clear and easy to use. *The Bluebook* has always been muddy and a torture to use. Yet it was what everyone had to master.

The *Bluebook* has faced challengers in recent years. The Association of Legal Writing Directors (ALWD) publishes a manual called the ***ALWD Guide to Legal Citation*** now in its fifth edition. It has made some headway but has not seized the mountaintop. The University of Chicago Law School publishes a much simpler guide, ***The University of Chicago Manual of Legal Citation*** known as the Maroonbook. Despite some avid lobbying by influential judges, it too has stalled out. Either may be used at your law school. Some state court systems have their own Style Manuals as well. But mostly you will be dealing with the *Bluebook*. Fortunately, Professor Patricia Hurley has made a dynamite video about it as part of the online lectures accompanying this book. It is as painless as such instruction can get.

c.   Restatements

We mention the ***Restatements*** because they play a major role in the way some first year courses are presented. You will find them cited most frequently in your Contracts and Torts classes. *Restatements* are not actually law in any jurisdiction. They are a powerful persuasive authority designed to assist the courts.

The *Restatement* movement dates back to the early part of the 20th Century. The *Restatements* are produced by the American Law Institute, a blue ribbon assemblage of lawyers, judges and professors. The idea was to bring order to the growing chaos of the common law by having the leading expert in each field read all relevant cases and then lay out the principles that governed them. The leading expert, called the Reporter, would bring his or her comments back to a committee of the A.L.I. for discussion. It took years to write the things, but all have been completed. Many have appeared in a second edition, and Torts is now appearing in its third. The *Restatement* represents the views of the best minds in the field. In some states they are cited a great deal; in other states they are not as powerful. Nowhere are they enacted into law.

If your casebook reprints a section of the *Restatement* it will be pulled out of context and hence may be very hard to understand. However, if you go to the *Restatement* itself you will find all manner of explanatory material. Just as with the difference between casebooks and actual case reports, the *Restatements* are designed for working lawyers and judges. They try to be clear, so go read the original if you want the whole picture. The *Restatements* are on Westlaw and Lexis in full text, and can be found in paper form at most law libraries.

d.   The Uniform Commercial Code

The *Uniform Commercial Code* (UCC) is a part of most first year Contracts classes. So what is it? As with the *Restatements*, the UCC is not really a source of law. It was drawn up by the American Law Institute and the National Conference of Commissioners on Uniform State Law. It was the brainchild of Professor Karl Llewellyn, one of the 20th Century's leading legal wild men. His idea was to provide a statute that could be adopted by each state in order to standardize commercial transactions. It also codified the progressive approach that many businesses had adopted when antiquated laws lacked flexibility. Persuading each state legislature to adopt it called for political savvy and enormous effort. It worked. The UCC has indeed been adopted, at least in part, by each state. The state legislatures may have made changes to it when they enacted it, so the language may differ from place to place in the real world. Even if the language is adopted in original form, courts in different states may interpret the very same language differently from one another. Finding out that unconscionability means one thing in California and another in New York is one of the joys of law school.

Often in your casebook you will be given a section of the UCC. Standing alone it can be hard to understand. However, if you look at the full text of the UCC you will find the drafters provide not just the text of the provision but also Official Comments, in which they try to explain what they are doing. The real-life UCC also has lots of examples to show the rule in application. So if you have trouble understanding a UCC provision, go check the actual UCC. It will provide lots of help, because it is designed for practitioners who are in search of an answer. The UCC is available in full-text on Westlaw and Lexis. There is a paper set called *Uniform Laws Annotated, Master Edition* which sits in almost every law library. There is no need to read the same passage in your casebook over and over, hoping that meaning can be found in the entrails. Do what a lawyer would do and get some help.

Advice on Surviving the First Semester of Law School

Some of you will love law school. For you each minute will be another scoop of ice cream in the hot fudge sundae of life. But for some of you law school will just make your head hurt. We have seen thousands of folks go through the experience, so here is our accumulated wisdom.

1. *Realize what is happening in class.* The classes in the first semester of the first year are about learning to think and analyze. The actual material covered is less important than the process of covering it. Some of you will have been good students all of your lives. You will be accustomed to reading the assigned material, mastering it, then getting it correct in class. Law school is not like that. We have already told you that most casebooks are structured to push (i.e., confuse) you, not to enlighten you. There are no correct answers to master. You will read cases at the borderline between established points. When the professor asks you a question in class, no matter what you say, or how brilliantly you say it, the professor can show you that you are wrong. This drives some folks nuts. They think that if they brief the case one more time, or do the reading again, they will see the truth. In first year courses there is no truth. There is only the process of thinking about the law. Remember that each case that you read had attorneys on each side making

cogent arguments. Do not despair when you cannot master the stuff. No one can. The day that you should really worry is the day that you think that it is all clear. Trust us, it is all murky. So let yourself go with the flow of the classroom discussion. Get background so you understand what is going on, but never feel bad if you get tripped up. It is a game. It is preparing you for later when instead of a well-meaning professor there will be a dagger-wielding opponent confronting you. So get in the mix and dare to look stupid. It makes law school a lot more fun.

2.   *Law school can be a bottomless pit.* You can allow your life to become pulled into the dark star of study groups and reading. We humbly suggest you do not allow this to happen. Those parts of your brain that were so valuable to you before you came to law school are still valuable. Keep them alive. There were plenty of things you liked to do before law school, and you should still do them. Go to movies, hang glide, play games, and be good to those who love you. Try to retain your sense of humor. There will be mighty forces in law school trying to scrape all that away. Do not let them win. Law school is for three years, and it is not an end in itself. It should be a corridor leading somewhere else.

We'll get down off our soapbox now. We assure you, it will all work out just fine.

CHAPTER 2

CASES

In Chapter 1 we provided an introduction to the materials that you will run into during your first year. In this Chapter we have to get serious and go straight into the heart of darkness. We are going to look at cases themselves. Just what are these things that you're going to spend so much time reading? We will take them apart by looking at them from four different directions:

- What is a case, and where does it come from? How is it produced?

- What is the doctrine of precedent and why should you care?

- How are cases put together? We will get a little mechanical and talk about the parts of the case that you will find when you read one.

- Where do you find cases, other than in your monster casebooks? We will talk about the formats in which cases are published, and the actual ways you will find them now and in the future.

Being the linear folks that we are, let's discuss these questions in order.

I. WHAT IS A CASE?

What is a case? In approaching this question we are going to assume that you are just as uninformed as we were when we went to law school. When we arrived at law school it felt as if we were walking in on Act II of a three-act play. Everyone else seemed to know what was going on. Of course, the fact is that most folks are lost. But no matter, we will start at the beginning and talk about where cases come from.

To understand what a case or judicial decision actually is, it helps to think first of the court systems that produce it. Professor Saffouri has created a terrific video on the structure of the court system. You should check it out. In what follows we will be able to provide more detail, but we will be limited to using text. You can pick your poison.

Since you are still reading this text, here is our best shot at telling you what is going on with cases. Think of courts in a pattern like that in our lovely three-part court diagram below.

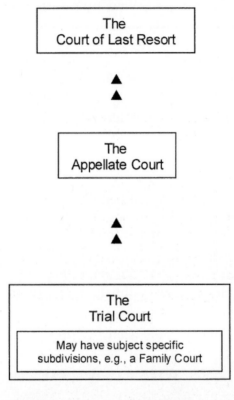

At the first level (where a case begins) you will see the trial court. At the second level there is an appellate court. Perched at the third level is a court of last resort. Why start with a model using generic titles for the levels? Because there are so many different jurisdictions. For starters, there are fifty states. Floating above the states, and sometimes tangling with them, is a federal system. There are various territories attached to the United States as well. Each of these jurisdictions has its own court system, just as it has its own legislative bodies, and its own administrative agencies with their own administrative rules and regulations. All of these different courts, bodies, or agencies use their own nomenclature—you can't remember all of them by heart, and you can't tell just by looking at the name of a court in a particular jurisdiction what it means. Only someone with the memory powers of a comic book hero could hope to memorize them all. Our solution is to use this generic functional model, and the functional model *does* apply in every jurisdiction. Wherever you go there will be some functional equivalent of the levels shown in this diagram.

Each jurisdiction is going to have some form of a trial court. Commonly, the trial court might be divided into segments. It may be divided according to the amount in dispute, like a Superior Court (that's what we call them in California). It might have a different name in your jurisdiction.[1] There may be subject specialty trial courts, like family courts, juvenile courts or drug courts. The set-up can change from jurisdiction to jurisdiction. What matters is that the trial court level is the first step in the judicial process. At this stage, there are two kinds of questions that might be presented in court, and about which decisions will be made by a judge and/or a jury: issues of law and issues of fact.

It is time for us to invoke that most venerable law school gambit, a hypothetical situation. Hypothetical situations are something that first year law professors just love to use in class. When one creates a hypothetical situation, one creates one's own world. So here's our hypothetical situation:

Let's say that one of your authors, let's say Bob, is preparing to give a lecture on legal research. He is thinking about how he wants to do a really great job. He wants to make you able to walk into the library, or to sit down at your computer terminal, and know what you are doing and, even better, why you are doing it. Engrossed in thought, (and if you ever saw Bob thinking you would know just how apt the term "engrossed" really is), he is crossing the street carrying a double latte when he is suddenly struck by a Lamborghini Diablo driven by Bruce Springsteen. Bob is injured. His leg is broken. As a result of the injury, he can't make it to the school to do his lecture. He loses his self-esteem. He loses sleep, weight, friends and hair. There might be

---

[1]   In New York that trial level court is generally called, oddly enough, the Supreme Court. There is also Family Court, Surrogates' Court, the Court of Claims, etc., at the trial level. This is what we meant when we said each jurisdiction has its own vocabulary.

any number of damages. (This is what your course in Torts will cover.)

Bob claims that Springsteen (hereinafter called the Boss) was driving at an excessive rate of speed, that he hit him while he was in the crosswalk and, instead of keeping his eyes on the road, he was texting. The Boss, however, claims that he was driving at a legal rate of speed and that a clearly drunken Bob leapt in front of his Lamborghini while screaming, "More money for education!" Now, given these two conflicting stories, what would happen in the real world? In the real universe in which we live, this matter would probably be settled by the relevant insurance companies. But in our hypothetical world, let's assume the parties couldn't work it out. We are in one of those rare situations where the conflict can't be resolved any other way, and everyone ends up in court.

The court we will end up in is a ***trial court***. The trial court resolves issues of law and issues of fact. When most of us think "court," we think of trial courts and we think of the resolution of issues of fact. (Think *The Good Wife, The Practice* and the Law half of *Law & Order.)* Remember Bob's claims about the crosswalk and the Boss's driving, and the Boss's contentions about his actions? Was he speeding? Was Bob inebriated? These are all issues of fact, and they will be determined by the ***trier of fact***. In popular culture we tend to think of the jury as the trier of fact, but judges can also make factual determinations. The casting for this role depends on the jurisdiction and the nature of the matter at hand. Sometimes the parties get a choice. The real point here is that the issues of fact are determined at the trial court level and they get frozen there. Please note that anytime we make a generalization there will be exceptions, and that is true here too, but, *in general,* you cannot appeal issues of fact: they are frozen. If the trier of fact, be it a jury or a judge, says that Bob was in the crosswalk, then he was in the crosswalk. He will be there for all time. If the trier of fact says the Boss was driving within the speed limit, then he was driving within the speed limit. Trial lawyers win or lose the factual battles and the results are locked in place. None of these factual determinations produce our written judicial opinion, but be patient, it is coming.

There is another kind of question that comes up at the trial court level: questions that concern *issues of law*. For example, if Bob wanted to introduce a witness who would say that they heard the Boss bragging afterwards that he had "knocked down another librarian," the Boss's attorney might jump up and say "I object. That's hearsay, you can't admit that." The judge would have to rule on this issue of (evidentiary) law—is the statement hearsay or not? Legal questions come in many forms. There might be a question of statutory interpretation or a common law problem. The exact nature of the legal issue doesn't really matter. What does matter is that we have an issue of law, and the *judge* makes the ruling on an issue of law. Issues of law *can* be appealed to a higher court, but the issues of fact *cannot*. The facts remain frozen and it is only the issues of law that travel up to higher courts. We know we are repeating ourselves, but this is important. Issues of law will be the subject of the cases that you will read. This is why so many of the cases that you read are so boring. They're boring because while at the trial court you might have all sorts of drama, with the Boss singing on the stand and the lawyers engaging in spectacular pyrotechnics. Those fireworks disappear on appeal. At the appellate level and above the facts are often leached out. The judges are focusing only on issues of law. The issues of law often involve interpreting their meaning but they are what they are.

Where do you appeal these issues of law decided at trial? You move to the next level of the court diagram: the appellate court. This level may have a different name in your jurisdiction, but the functional equivalent will be there. At the appellate level a court might have to take a case, or the court may have some discretion. It varies. (It always varies. Sorry!) Because the appellate level focuses on issues of law, everything changes. You don't have witnesses, you don't have juries. What you have are lawyers on each side. Those lawyers prepare written briefs which set out their point of law trying to convince the court to rule their way. The lawyers probably will get a chance to make an oral argument in front of the court. At most law schools this kind of appellate argument is exactly what you are going to learn and practice in Moot Court.

The appellate level may have one judge or there may be three judges. The judge (or judges) considers the briefs and oral arguments in order to reach a decision. In many matters the appellate court will not produce a written decision. They may just affirm or deny the ruling of the trial court. But in some matters the appellate court will decide to write an opinion. If the appellate court does decide to write an opinion and decides to publish it, *then* we have a judicial opinion. *A judicial opinion is the written resolution of issues of law usually from an appellate court or higher.* There will be exceptions to this generalization, too, because in the federal system the trial courts (Federal District Courts) serve a variety of functions, and oftentimes Federal District Courts will produce written opinions, but for now, let's stick with the general definition of a written resolution of an issue of law by the appellate court or higher.

Do all appellate opinions get published? No, not by a long shot. Every jurisdiction, every state, every one of the Federal Courts of Appeal has its own rules as to what gets published. A very large number of written opinions are not designated for entry into the stream of precedent. The resolution of our hypothetical matter will be important to the Boss and to Bob. They certainly want to know who won, but the judge may decide that this particular decision doesn't make any new law and does not merit entry into the stream of precedent. By not publishing an opinion, the Court can limit the application of its decision to only Bob and the Boss. The question of what gets published is actually quite a hot topic these days. All you need to know for now is that most decisions at the appellate level don't get published. The ones that do make it through the hoop of publication are part of what you will find on Westlaw, Lexis, and Bloomberg Law and in the case reporter volumes.

Now, what if the parties still want to fight after the appellate court has rendered its decision? In every jurisdiction there is another level of appeal: the *court of last resort*.

In most jurisdictions the court of last resort is called the Supreme Court.[2] The court of last resort level almost always has discretionary jurisdiction. That means they don't have to take every case. You have to ask them to consider your question of law, and it is up to them whether they will or not. There may be legislation or constitutional provisions that require the court of last resort in a particular jurisdiction to take a particular case, but in general it is up to them. The Supreme Court of the United States has thousands upon thousands of requests every year, importuning them to take cases, but they take only a few. (It is called "granting certiorari" or "granting cert." to the cognoscenti). This form of discretion is going to be the case in almost every jurisdiction.

Let's assume that the Supreme Court of California, where Bob lives, does take the case of *Berring v. Springsteen*. At the court of last resort lawyers once again will write briefs. These briefs again focus on the issues of law that are in play. A court of last resort may accept only one of the issues of law you'd like to appeal, or they may accept several for argument. Once the written briefs are submitted, oral argument may be scheduled. Lawyers who are specialists in appellate advocacy will present ideas to the court and answer questions. There is variation (what a shock!) among jurisdictions, but courts of last resort tend to have five, seven or maybe nine judges. This group of justices will then mull over the matter and decide it. Once again we ask the question, does everything that such a court writes get published?

For a court of last resort the general rule is *yes*. In every jurisdiction the court of last resort is so important, that it does tend to publish everything. But not every matter that they take under advisement is going to result in a written opinion. All they *have* to do is affirm the decision from below or overrule the decision from below, which doesn't necessarily require a written opinion. A single word, "affirmed" for instance, disposes of the matter between the Boss and Bob, and it makes the appellate court's opinion the last word on the subject. But in most situations when they have taken the matter and have heard the

---

[2]   However, this is not invariably true. For example, New York calls its Court of Last Resort the Court of Appeals. You know New Yorkers, always trying to keep you on your toes.

arguments, the court of last resort will issue an opinion. That's what this thing called a case, or a judicial opinion, is: the written resolution of issues of law, usually from the appellate level and above. While many matters will not result in a judicial opinion, when a decision *is* produced and designated for publication you will find it on Westlaw, Lexis, Bloomberg Law and in the printed judicial reports as well as in a variety of other places.[3]

Because the judicial panels at the appellate level and above are composed of groups of people, there can be disagreement among the judges. Our tradition is for one judge to write the opinion of the court for the whole panel. There is a name at the beginning of the opinion, as in "Levy, J." The "J" stands for Judge or Justice. When Bob was brand new law student he thought that all judges must be named Jim, John and Jane until someone explained that to him. The judge writing an opinion will not just name a winner. If an opinion is written, it is done because the court wants to explain *why* the winner won. Judicial reasoning is important for the doctrine of precedent, which we will cover in Section 2. Much of your time as a first year student will be spent trying to parse out what judges mean in these opinions. It is no simple task. Opinions can run for many pages, and they can be strewn with speculation on everything under the sun. The Supreme Court case that we will use as an exemplar throughout the book, *Gonzales v. Raich*, includes among many other things, the history of marijuana in California. But the only thing that represents the law is that part where the judge resolves an issue of law. The rest is called "dicta." More on that later.

Sometimes within a multi-judge panel there is disagreement. Our model case, *Gonzales v. Raich* is just such a case. If so, then the opinion discussed in the paragraph above is dubbed the "majority opinion." If one of the judges agrees with the result—she thinks that the right person prevailed should—but does not agree with the reasoning used in the opinion, she can decide to write a separate opinion. This is called a

---

[3] There is some weirdness here. An opinion is officially published only if the issuing Court deems it so. Often a Court will write an opinion addressed to the parties, but will not designate the opinion for publication. But information vendors like Lexis and Westlaw can gain access to such opinions and may load them into their database. Thus you may read an opinion which is not published. There is even a printed West set called the Federal Appendix which contains printed unpublished opinions. Printed unpublished opinions! You just cannot tell us that legal research is not funny.

"concurring" opinion. In it the judge will say why she agrees that the Boss should win, but that she has an entirely different rationale for doing so. This weakens the power of the majority opinion of the court. In *Gonzales v. Raich*, the late Justice Scalia authors just such a concurrence.

Sometimes there will be judges who disagree with the result entirely. Such a judge thinks Bob should have won. This judge might write an opinion explaining why the majority of the court (or, even the concurring judge) is wrong and why. Such an opinion is referred to as a "dissenting" opinion. *Gonzales v. Raich* features several dissenting opinions. There used to be a tradition of trying to avoid dissents, but in recent years they have been very prevalent. The Supreme Court of the United States decisions often feature a majority opinion, a concurring opinion or two and a dissent or two. Some of the dissents can be quite harsh. The late Justice Scalia was renowned for his colorful dissents. You will even find judges or justices who concur in part and dissent in part. Our all-time favorite case for this purpose is *Regents of the Univ. of Cal. v. Bakke.*[4] This was a case about affirmative action in the 1970s. It made it to the Supreme Court of the United States and each of the nine Justices wrote an opinion. Making sense out of something like that—who agrees with what and why—is a true art form. It is an art form that you are going to be studying this year. Our chart below sums up the types of opinions.

---

[4]   *Regents of the Univ. of Cal. v. Bakke,* 43 U.S. 265, 98 S.Ct. 2733, 57 L.Ed. 2d 750 (1978). Frequently you will find the full citation to a reference in the footnotes.

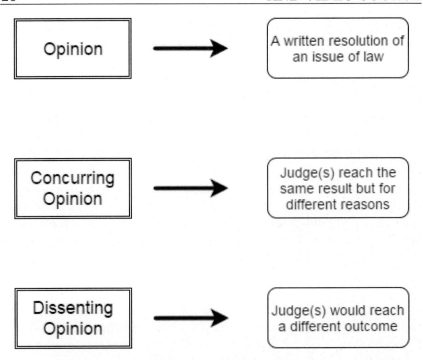

One of the most important things to keep in mind when you are reading judicial decisions is that they are not mystery stories. This is not like a Lee Child or Elmore Leonard novel where there is a surprise ending. The judges have ruminated and argued about the case. Various drafts of opinions may have passed back and forth. It can be a very political process. The case that you are reading is not a balanced account of the arguments made in the lawyers' briefs, it is the strongest statement of the winning position. This is why if you read a dissent in a case, it often sounds like a different matter entirely. The author of the opinion handcrafts it. Keep that in mind. Bob has made a video about reading a case and trying to understand how a judge operates. Check it out.

There is one more variation worth noting. Sometimes the court does not want to have an individual write the opinion. In that case they can issue a *per curiam* opinion.[5] In a *per curiam*

---

[5] *Per curiam* is Latin. The law is still strewn with Latin phrases and outmoded expressions. When you encounter these you must look them up. Honest. Learning these things is important and may save you from getting gutted in class. Just this once we'll translate for you: *per curiam* means, "by the court."

opinion the whole court is writing. This is usually done in cases that are special. It might be something really simple, it might be something really complex, but in either case a *per curiam* decision is not as strong in precedential value.

Now that we've looked at what a case is, we want to look at why cases are important. That means looking at the doctrine of precedent.

II. THE DOCTRINE OF PRECEDENT

The doctrine of precedent descends to us from the English common law system. The United States is a common law jurisdiction. So are the nations that comprise the British Commonwealth and former colonies. The other great legal system that sprang from Western European roots is the Civil Law system. The Civil Law system is founded on Roman Law principles and can be found in Western Europe and countries like China and Japan.

Common law jurisdictions are distinguished by the fact that we believe that courts make primary law, that is, that the decisions of the courts can be primary source material. Intuitively it's easy to understand why legislation should be viewed as a primary source of law. Our elected representatives create legislation under our Constitution. It's also intuitively easy to understand why administrative rules and regulations should be viewed as a primary source of law, because they are created under delegations of power from the legislative bodies we elect.

But why should the decisions of courts be viewed as law? Shouldn't judges just interpret the law? In many jurisdictions judges aren't even elected. At the federal level where they are most important, they are not elected and they are appointed for life. There have been federal judges who were sent to prison who still drew their salary. Why should we let these non-elected representatives make law? The classic response is, they ***don't*** make law—instead judges reveal law. When a judge rules on an issue of law, he or she isn't making it up, instead he or she is saying, "Here's what the law is, and what we all know it to be. There has never been a rule on this point before, so I am telling you what it is. But it is not me making this up, it was already there." This may strike you as so belabored as to be ridiculous, but there you are.

There is a doctrinal basis for it that derives from the concept of the "natural law." Whole courses are taught about this matter, but we plan to summarize it in a few sentences. Buckle your seat belt. There used to be a belief that there was a perfect system of immutable principles floating up in the sky above us. It was based on the Judeo-Christian belief in a natural law decreed in Heaven. The theory ran that the common law was man's approximation of the perfection of natural law. The perfect law is out there, the judge just has to find it. Although most scholars don't believe in this theory anymore, it still informs our common law system. The judge does not make the law, she reveals part of this perfect system.

That is why the judge's reasoning is very important, and why it's so important for the majority opinion to set out its reasons. Every time an opinion resolves an issue of law, that issue of law is resolved as a primary source of legal authority in the relevant jurisdiction. The decision binds the courts below that court in the same jurisdiction, and courts at the same level into the future. They have to follow that particular decision. The law has now been revealed. We will see in Chapter 4, when we look at citators, that a court can change its mind over time, but they don't like to do that. Too many reversals erode public confidence.

Therefore, the reasoning of an appellate level court is very important. If a court finds a particular legal issue to fall out a particular way, they are creating something that future legal researchers can use, something that future courts must consider. A lawyer can say "Look, in the past this has been decided this way and we can draw an analogy to it. There is the law." Of course, the lawyer for the other side is going to find other cases and arrive at different analogies. In matters that reach the appellate level of adjudication there will always be at least two sides to each issue.

This process of building structures of analogies to points of law is what's going on in the first year classroom. First year professors try to make you understand what these analogies mean and how they can be used. Because of the doctrine of precedent, the majority opinion is going to be crafted in a way that will not just resolve the matter between Bruce Springsteen and Bob. (We don't know about you, but by this point we're pulling for the Boss.) The reasoning of the court in making its decisions might be important to generations of people following after them. Now, not to say that the classic songs of Bruce Springsteen won't be important for generations of folks who follow us, or that this book won't be important to generations of law students yet unborn, but I'd say the odds are better that the legal point and the precedential stream is going to outlast all of us.

Keep in mind all that good stuff from Part 1. Only the written resolution of the issue of law counts as precedent. A judge could write an opinion resolving the great Springsteen/Berring controversy that discussed the pathetic state of popular music and the annoying personal habits of law professors. That will all be dicta. Only when the court resolves an issue of law will precedent kick in.

III. THE PARTS OF AN OPINION

We shall now get mechanical and look at the parts of the judicial decision that you are going to encounter. While there is inevitable variation, the parts are pretty generic. You will find them whether you use Westlaw, Lexis, case reporter volumes or a court website. First we will describe the various parts of a case, then we will show you what they look like using the case of *Gonzales v. Raich* as an example. The plan is to use this case as the reference for all of the analysis that follows. We've printed out some screenshots of pages from that case from both Westlaw and Lexis and put them at the end of the chapter and marked them up for you, pointing out the parts of the case we're about to describe (and a few others besides, added by the editors at Westlaw and Lexis). If you prefer to see these examples explained by a live human, check out the video. The same case is used throughout them as well.

a. The Caption

The caption is the name of the case. In our example that is *Gonzales v. Raich*. You will note when you look at the example that the names of the parties are actually longer than *Gonzales v. Raich.* There are special rules for how one correctly abbreviates the caption. There may be a whole bunch of people suing a whole bunch of people, or perhaps a corporation is suing someone. (This is America, everyone is suing someone.) So we need a standard way to abbreviate case captions. *The Uniform System of Citation,* that hateful book of citations described in Chapter 1 and brilliantly set out by Professor Hurley in her video and often called by its nickname, *The Bluebook,* is the guide.

The Bluebook, provides the rules for how to construct the citation. If you are in a school that uses the *ALWD Manual,* you can use that for the same result.

Typically you call the first party the plaintiff and the second party the defendant, that's one we all learned from watching television shows. Law students use the pi (π) sign for plaintiff and the delta (A) for defendant. No one knows why, so feel free to make up your own rationale. Depending on the jurisdiction, you might find the first party called the appellant and the second the appellee. In some jurisdictions, the first party is the petitioner and the second is the respondent. It varies both by jurisdiction and the procedural posture of the case.

You should be careful about the order of the parties' names. Remember that we are reading cases from appellate level courts or above. Sometimes as the case works its way through the system, the parties reverse their position. If Bob sued the Boss at the trial court level and won, he would be the party who was appealing. (Feel free to make your own joke here.) When this happens in some jurisdictions they switch the order of the party names. In some cases they might actually change parties' names. That happened in *Gonzales v. Raich.* When the matter began, John Ashcroft was the Attorney General of the United States. So the caption was *Raich v. Ashcroft.* While the case was working its way through the system, Attorney General Ashcroft resigned and Alberto Gonzales replaced him. So the matter became *Raich v. Gonzales.* Since Raich won at Court of Appeals, the parties switched their spots on either side of the "v" at the Supreme Court level. Voila: *Gonzales v. Raich.* Each jurisdiction has its own rules.

b.   The Docket Number

Each case has a docket number. That number is an alphanumeric assigned by the court for internal filing purposes. If you want to go look at an actual case file, you might need the docket number. Docket numbers are also excellent hooks to use when doing an online search. You have to be careful when you use them as you have to get it right, but they are unique so they yield good results. Docket numbers may grow even more important as new format-neutral citation systems are built. (Don't worry if that last sentence reads like so much ancient Greek, you will find out what it means later.) But as of now those don't exist most places so you *can* worry about it later.

c.   Syllabus

A syllabus is a summary of the case. Most decisions will have only the syllabus written by editors who work for a for-profit publisher. Though these people are faceless and nameless, they are practiced and skilled. Someone has read the case for you, and then prepared an abstract of it. The syllabus is usually very direct. It says this case came from here, it's about this, and here's how the decision came out. Quite an aid to the researcher in search of quick guidance. In our examples at the end of this chapter, you'll note that the editors at Lexis and Westlaw have written a summary of the case <u>and</u> there is a syllabus from the Reporter of The Supreme Court of the United States. The Supreme Court is so important that it has a scholarly Court Reporter who writes a very detailed syllabus for each case. Just compare the three syllabi. (How's that for a $10 word?) The official Court Reporter is much longer. The ones by editors at Westlaw and Lexis are shorter but still helpful. These good folks are trying to tell you what happened. This is not primary source material, it is not the law itself, but it is a summary of it. For a first year student reading the syllabus of a case is like reading *Cliff Notes*. Sometimes even the syllabus will be hard to read because it might be very technical, but it's there to help you, to guide you. The syllabus is also important because in Westlaw or Lexis, the syllabus provides a kind of normalized language that can help you if you're terms and connectors searching, and make you more productive.

d. Headnotes

Almost every case that you find will have headnotes. What is a headnote? Headnotes are produced by an editor who reads the case for you and attempts to extract and summarize each point of law that is resolved in the case. The editor may work for the court or for a publisher like Westlaw or Lexis. If there is an editor at the court, you might get her headnotes and also those done by the commercial publisher. The editor will summarize in the headnote what the court has decided. Commercial headnote writers strain to write with great precision and accuracy. The number of headnotes can vary considerably. You may find dozens in front of an opinion. Compare the *United States Supreme Court Reporter* version of a case with the same case on Westlaw and Lexis. You will see wholly different headnotes. Writing these things is an art form, not a science.

The headnote will carry a number, or it will be hyperlinked online so that you can go to the section of the text that the editor was reading when she wrote the headnote. This helps you focus your research and it also lets you check on whether you agree with her or not. Some research instructors advise folks never to rely on headnotes. After all, headnotes are the work of someone who stands between you and the words of the court. Except in Ohio (Bob is a proud Buckeye by birth) headnotes are not statements of the law. So you should not rely on them. But trust us, if some night you have to read three hundred cases and you can consume no more caffeine, headnotes can help.

Each headnote in Lexis and Westlaw carries a subject tag as well. There are highly articulated subject search systems at the other end of these links. More on that in the next chapter.

e. Names of Counsel

The names of the lawyers who carried the appeal forward are listed. If you are really puzzled about why a case came out the way it did, try e-mailing the winning side. This advice may seem deranged but it can work. Remember that the opinion is often resolving issues raised in the briefs. Reading the briefs filed by counsel opens a treasure trove of research hooks. Both online systems will oftentimes lead you to the briefs. To

understand an opinion it really can help to know what the
questions were. Remember, the winners are usually happier to
chat than the losers.[6]

f.   The Opinion

We discussed the forms of opinions in the previous section.
When you are looking at our example of *Gonzales v. Raich* at the
end of this chapter, note that there is a majority opinion, a
concurring opinion and several dissents. In one of the videos Bob
is going to ask you to read the entire thing so that he can discuss
how to read a case. You might try it now. You will learn about
the history of the legal status of marijuana, the story of
American drug laws and the wheat market. Most of it is dicta,
but it has its moments.

IV.   FORMATS OF CASES

Other than the bits and pieces of cases in your casebooks,
most students who read this book will read cases on Westlaw
and Lexis. At this point in time, Westlaw and Lexis offer full-
text libraries that include every case that can be found in the
paper reporters, and more. Some of you may share the love of
the printed page that we have, and your law library will still be
there to support you if you do. But the world of legal research
has gone digital. If you keep the question of your case's relevant
jurisdiction in mind, and recall our three-part court diagram,
you can pretty much figure out what you have in hand.

Many lawyers trained in the past, (and that may include
someone for whom you will work), were trained in the paper
world of cases. Citation is built around the paper world of cases.
So we wish to give the printed volumes their due. If you want a
lot of detail go to one of the longer research books. What follows
is our survival guide approach.

---

[6] Some who reviewed the manuscript of this book thought that this advice was
deranged. It may well be deranged but we have done it. In the 2001–2002 academic year
Bob called the lawyers who appeared in two cases in the Contracts casebook that he was
using. The cases appeared nonsensical. The lawyers were happy to explain why. So, it
may be deranged, but it is effective.

a.   Reading a Case Citation

In the world of paper, case citations followed a standard format. Here it is for the *Raich* case:

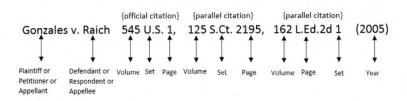

If there is an official citation, it goes first. If there is a citation to the West National Reporter system, it goes second. If there is a third relevant cite it can be added as well. The second citation (and any that follow it) is called a parallel citation. The volume number, set, page number formula is very reliable. There are variations, but who cares?

b.   Official Reports

If a jurisdiction publishes its own decisions and deems them to be the official form of the judicial report, you cite to them first. About half of the states have official reports. At the federal level there is an official report of Supreme Court opinions, *U.S. Reports*, but there are none for the lower federal courts. In many jurisdictions that have official reports, they come out slowly; in other places they are timely. The headnoting in official reports usually is less intensive and the headnotes do not plug into larger research systems. The bound volumes of judicial reports are preceded by paperbound pamphlets called advance sheets. Advance sheets feature the same pagination as the eventual bound volume so that you can cite to them with confidence.

c.   The National Reporter System

Thomson Reuters produces the *National Reporter System (NRS)*. This set of books divides the United States into seven regions and two state volumes for New York and California and prints all the judicial reports or cases that are published by the states in the relevant regions. The regions were created at the end of the 19th Century so they are a bit odd (few folks think of Oklahoma as a Pacific state these days) but it does not really matter. Think of the regions as arbitrary divisions. There is a special segment of the system for California and for New York as those two states were producing too many opinions and were overwhelming their regional reporter. The solution was to put only the opinions of the courts of last resort in California and New York into the relevant regional reporter and to put all appellate decisions into the *California Reporter* and the *New York Supplement,* respectively.

There is also a federal component to the NRS. United States Supreme Court cases go into the *Supreme Court Reporter,* cases from the United States Courts of Appeal go into the *Federal Reporter,* and cases from the United States District Courts go into *Federal Supplement.* As there is no official report of lower federal court cases, citation to the West NRS volumes was the only way to present information. As we move to a world of digital information, this will change, but it is changing slowly and most folks still use NRS citations. Westlaw and Lexis will note on the screen the relevant page you would be reading if you were reading the case in the NRS. This is called star paging. It might seem quaint to you that everyone is still citing to the printed volume when almost no one is using it, but we do a lot of funny things in the law. This will not be the oddest.

Below is a table of the National Reporter System.

Title of Publication	Cases reported from . . .
Federal Supplement	Federal District Courts
Federal Reporter	Federal Courts of Appeal (the Circuit Courts)
Supreme Court Reporter	U.S. Supreme Court
Atlantic	Connecticut, Delaware, the District of Columbia, Maine, Maryland, New Hampshire, New Jersey, Pennsylvania, Rhode Island, and Vermont

Southern	Alabama, Florida, Louisiana, and Mississippi
South Eastern	Georgia, North Carolina, South Carolina, Virginia, and West Virginia
South Western	Arkansas, Kentucky, Missouri, Tennessee, and Texas
North Eastern	Illinois, Indiana, Massachusetts, New York, Ohio
North Western	Iowa, Michigan, Minnesota, Nebraska, North Dakota, South Dakota, and Wisconsin
Pacific	Alaska, Arizona, Colorado, Hawaii, Idaho, Kansas, Montana, Nevada, New Mexico, Oklahoma, Oregon, Utah, Washington, and Wyoming
California Reporter	California Supreme Court and appellate courts
New York Supplement	New York Court of Appeals, Appellate Division of the State Supreme Court, and additional state courts

There are many other places to find cases. Many courts now publish their decisions on a website. Some non-profit groups collect cases to make them freely available. There are law libraries that make the same effort. But the reality in 2016 is that the National Reporter System, Lexis and Westlaw are the only complete sets, with all the features discussed above and which are trusted by researchers.

SUMMARY

We have tried to introduce you to the world of cases. It will seem like a lot of noise, but it will help if you can distance yourself and think about the cases beyond your casebooks. You will work with them in practice. It is good to know them now.

What follows are a couple of looks at the parts of a case as shown in *Gonzales v. Raich*. The first set of screenshots are from Westlaw, followed by Lexis. Enjoy!

Illustrations

GONZALES v. RAICH: WESTLAW

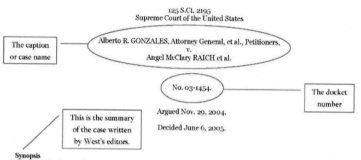

KeyCite Yellow Flag - Negative Treatment
Declined to Extend by National Federation of Independent Business v. Sebelius, U.S., June 28, 2012

125 S.Ct. 2195
Supreme Court of the United States

| The caption or case name |

Alberto R. GONZALES, Attorney General, et al., Petitioners,
v.
Angel McClary RAICH et al.

No. 03-1454.

| The docket number |

Argued Nov. 29, 2004.

Decided June 6, 2005.

| This is the summary of the case written by West's editors. |

Synopsis

Background: Users and growers of marijuana for medical purposes under California Compassionate Use Act sought declaration that Controlled Substances Act (CSA) was unconstitutional as applied to them. The United States District Court for the Northern District of California, Martin J. Jenkins, J., 248 F.Supp.2d 918, denied plaintiffs' motion for preliminary injunction. Plaintiffs appealed. The United States Court of Appeals for the Ninth Circuit, Pregerson, Circuit Judge, 352 F.3d 1222, reversed and remanded. Certiorari was granted.

[Holding:] The Supreme Court, Justice Stevens, held that application of CSA provisions criminalizing manufacture, distribution, or possession of marijuana to intrastate growers and users of marijuana for medical purposes did not violate Commerce Clause.

Vacated and remanded.

Justice Scalia concurred in judgment and filed opinion.

Justice O'Connor dissented and filed opinion in which Chief Justice Rehnquist and Justice Thomas joined in part.

Justice Thomas dissented and filed opinion.

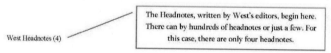

| The Headnotes, written by West's editors, begin here. There can by hundreds of headnotes or just a few. For this case, there are only four headnotes. |

West Headnotes (4)

[1]   **Commerce** ⟡ Federal Offenses and Prosecutions
       Controlled Substances ⟡ Validity

       Application of Controlled Substances Act (CSA) provisions criminalizing manufacture, distribution, or possession of marijuana to intrastate growers and users of marijuana for medical purposes, as otherwise authorized by California Compassionate Use Act, did not exceed Congress' authority under Commerce Clause; prohibition of intrastate growth and use of marijuana was rationally related to regulation of interstate commerce in marijuana. U.S.C.A. Const. Art. 1, § 8, cl. 3; Comprehensive Drug Abuse Prevention and Control Act of 1970, §§ 401(a)(1), 404(a), 21 U.S.C.A. §§ 841(a)(1), 844(a); West's Ann.Cal.Health & Safety Code § 11362.5.

501 Cases that cite this headnote

[2]   **Commerce**⟊Activities Affecting Interstate Commerce

Commerce Clause grants Congress power to regulate purely local activities that are part of economic class of activities that have substantial effect on interstate commerce. U.S.C.A. Const. Art. 1, § 8, cl. 3.

372 Cases that cite this headnote

[3]   **Constitutional Law**⟊Determination of Propriety of Classification

Where class of activities is regulated and that class is within reach of federal power, courts have no power to excise, as trivial, individual instances of class.

58 Cases that cite this headnote

[4]   **Commerce**⟊Commerce Among the States

State action cannot circumscribe Congress' plenary commerce power. U.S.C.A. Const. Art. 1, § 8, cl. 3.

93 Cases that cite this headnote

> The Syllabus, written by the Reporter of Decisions at the U.S. Supreme Court begins here. We've edited this down, too.

West Codenotes

> Star paging

Negative Treatment Vacated
21 U.S.C. § 841(a)(1)

**2196 *1 *Syllabus*

California's Compassionate Use Act authorizes limited marijuana use for medicinal purposes. Respondents Raich and Monson are California residents who both use doctor-recommended marijuana for serious medical conditions. After federal Drug Enforcement Administration agents seized and destroyed all six of Monson's cannabis plants, respondents brought this action seeking injunctive and declaratory relief prohibiting the enforcement of the federal Controlled Substances Act (CSA) to the extent it prevents them from possessing, obtaining, or manufacturing cannabis for their personal medical use. Respondents claim that enforcing the CSA against them would violate the Commerce Clause and other constitutional provisions. The District Court denied respondents' motion for a preliminary injunction, but the Ninth Circuit reversed, finding that they had demonstrated a strong likelihood of success on the claim that the CSA is an unconstitutional exercise of Congress' Commerce Clause authority as applied to the intrastate, noncommercial cultivation and possession of cannabis for personal medical purposes as recommended by a patient's physician pursuant to valid California state law. The court relied heavily on *United States v. Lopez*, 514 U.S. 549, 115 S.Ct. 1624, 131 L.Ed.2d 626, and *United States v. Morrison*, 529 U.S. 598, 120 S.Ct. 1740, 146 L.Ed.2d 658, to hold that this separate class of purely local activities was beyond the reach of federal power.

*2 *Held:* Congress' Commerce Clause authority includes the power to prohibit the local cultivation and use of marijuana in compliance with California law. Pp. 2201-2215.

(a) For the purposes of consolidating various drug laws into a comprehensive statute, providing meaningful regulation over legitimate sources of drugs to prevent diversion into illegal channels, and strengthening law enforcement tools ****2197** against international and interstate drug trafficking, Congress enacted the Comprehensive Drug Abuse Prevention and Control Act of 1970, Title II of which is the CSA. To effectuate the statutory goals, Congress devised a closed regulatory system making it unlawful to manufacture, distribute, dispense, or possess any controlled substance except as authorized by the CSA. 21 U.S.C. §§ 841(a)(1), 844(a). All controlled substances are classified into five schedules, § 812, based on their accepted medical uses, and their potential for abuse, and their psychological and physical effects on the body, §§ 811, 812. Marijuana is classified as a Schedule I substance, § 812(c), based on its high potential for abuse, no accepted medical use, and no accepted safety for use in medically supervised treatment, § 812(b)(1). This classification renders the manufacture, distribution, or possession of marijuana a criminal offense. §§ 841(a)(1), 844(a). Pp. 2201-2204.

(b) Congress' power to regulate purely local activities that are part of an economic "class of activities" that have a substantial effect on interstate commerce is firmly established. See, *e.g.*, *Perez v. United States*, 402 U.S. 146, 151, 91 S.Ct. 1357, 28 L.Ed.2d 686. If Congress decides that the " 'total incidence' " of a practice poses a threat to a national market, it may regulate the entire class. See, *e.g.*, *id.*, at 154-155, 91 S.Ct. 1357. Of particular relevance here is *Wickard v. Filburn*, 317 U.S. 111, 127-128, 63 S.Ct. 82, 87 L.Ed. 122, where, in rejecting the appellee farmer's contention that Congress' admitted power to regulate the production of wheat for commerce did not authorize federal regulation of wheat production intended wholly for the appellee's own consumption, the Court established that Congress can regulate purely intrastate activity that is not itself "commercial," *i.e.*, not produced for sale, if it concludes that failure to regulate that class of activity would undercut the regulation of the interstate market in that commodity. The similarities between this case and *Wickard* are striking. In both cases, the regulation is squarely within Congress' commerce power because production of the commodity meant for home consumption, be it wheat or marijuana, has a substantial effect on supply and demand in the national market for that commodity. In assessing the scope of Congress' Commerce Clause authority, the Court need not determine whether respondents' activities, taken in the aggregate, substantially affect interstate commerce in fact, but only whether a "rational basis" exists for so concluding. *E.g.*, *Lopez*, 514 U.S., at 557, 115 S.Ct. 1624. Given the enforcement ***3** difficulties that attend distinguishing between marijuana cultivated locally and marijuana grown elsewhere, 21 U.S.C. § 801(5), and concerns about diversion into illicit channels, the Court has no difficulty concluding that Congress had a rational basis for believing that failure to regulate the intrastate manufacture and possession of marijuana would leave a gaping hole in the CSA. Pp. 2204-2209.

(c) Respondents' heavy reliance on *Lopez* and *Morrison* overlooks the larger context of modern-era Commerce Clause jurisprudence preserved by those cases, while also reading those cases far too broadly. The statutory challenges at issue there were markedly different from the challenge here. Respondents ask the Court to excise individual applications of a concededly valid comprehensive statutory scheme. In contrast, in both *Lopez* and *Morrison*, the parties asserted that a particular statute or provision fell outside Congress' commerce power in its entirety. This distinction is pivotal for the Court has often reiterated that "[w]here the class of activities is regulated and that class is within the reach of federal power, the ****2198** courts have no power 'to excise, as trivial, individual instances' of the class." *Perez*, 402 U.S., at 154, 91 S.Ct. 1357. Moreover, the Court emphasized that the laws at issue in *Lopez* and *Morrison* had nothing to do with "commerce" or any sort of economic enterprise. See *Lopez*, 514 U.S., at 561, 115 S.Ct. 1624; *Morrison*, 529 U.S., at 610, 120 S.Ct. 1740. In contrast, the CSA regulates quintessentially economic activities: the production, distribution, and consumption of commodities for which there is an established, and lucrative, interstate market. Prohibiting the intrastate possession or manufacture of an article of commerce is a rational means of regulating commerce in that product. The Ninth Circuit cast doubt on the CSA's constitutionality by isolating a distinct class of activities that it held to be beyond the reach of federal power: the intrastate, noncommercial cultivation, possession, and use of marijuana for personal medical purposes on the advice of a physician and in accordance with state law. However, Congress clearly acted rationally in determining that this subdivided class of activities is an essential part of the larger regulatory scheme. The case comes down to the claim that a locally cultivated product that is used domestically rather than sold on the open market is not subject to federal regulation. Given the CSA's findings and the undisputed magnitude of the commercial market for marijuana, *Wickard* and its progeny foreclose that claim. Pp. 2209-2215.

352 F.3d 1222, vacated and remanded.

STEVENS, J., delivered the opinion of the Court, in which KENNEDY, SOUTER, GINSBURG, and BREYER, JJ., joined. SCALIA, J., filed an opinion concurring in the judgment, *post*, p. 2215. O'CONNOR, J., filed a dissenting opinion, in which REHNQUIST, C. J., and THOMAS, J., joined as to all but Part III, *post*, p. 2220. THOMAS, J., filed a dissenting opinion, *post*, p. 2229.

Attorneys and Law Firms —————————— Name of Counsel

Robert A. Raich, Oakland, David M. Michael, The DeMartini Historical, Landmark Building, San Francisco, CA, Randy E. Barnett, Boston University, School of Law, Boston, MA, Robert A. Long, Jr., Counsel of Record, Heidi C. Doerhoff, Joshua D. Greenberg, Covington & Burling, Washington, DC, for Respondents.

Paul D. Clement, Acting Solicitor General, Counsel of Record, Peter D. Keisler, Assistant Attorney General, Edwin S. Kneedler, Deputy Solicitor General, Lisa S. Blatt, Assistant to the Solicitor General, Mark B. Stern, Alisa B. Klein, Mark T. Quinlivan, Attorneys, Department of Justice, Washington, D.C., Brief for the Petitioners.

Opinion ————————————————————

Justice STEVENS delivered the opinion of the Court.

> The Opinion begins here, after the name of the judge.

*5 California is one of at least nine States that authorize the use of marijuana for medicinal purposes.[1] The question presented ****2199** in this case is whether the power vested in Congress by Article I, § 8, of the Constitution "[t]o make all Laws which shall be necessary and proper for carrying into Execution" its authority to "regulate Commerce with foreign Nations, and among the several States" includes the power to prohibit the local cultivation and use of marijuana in compliance with California law.

GONZALES v. RAICH: LEXIS

Gonzales v. Raich

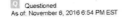
The caption
or case name

Supreme Court of the United States

November 29, 2004, Argued; June 6, 2005, Decided

No. 03-1454

The docket
number

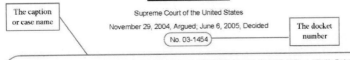

Reporter: 545 U.S. 1; 125 S. Ct. 2195; 162 L. Ed. 2d 1; 2005 U.S. LEXIS 4656; 73 U.S.L.W. 4407; 18 Fla. L. Weekly Fed. S 327

ALBERTO R. GONZALES, ATTORNEY GENERAL, et al., Petitioners v. ANGEL McCLARY RAICH et al.

Subsequent History: On remand at *Raich v. Gonzales, 500 F.3d 850, 2007 U.S. App. LEXIS 5834 (9th Cir. Cal., Mar. 14, 2007)*

Prior History: ON WRIT OF CERTIORARI TO THE UNITED STATES COURT OF APPEALS FOR THE NINTH CIRCUIT.

Raich v. Ashcroft, 352 F.3d 1222, 2003 U.S. App. LEXIS 25317 (9th Cir. Cal., 2003)

Disposition: Vacated and remanded.

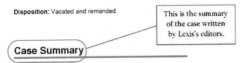
This is the summary
of the case written
by Lexis's editors.

Case Summary

Procedural Posture

Respondents, claiming a violation of the *Commerce Clause*, sought injunctive and declaratory relief prohibiting enforcement of the federal Controlled Substances Act (CSA), *21 U.S.C.S. § 801 et seq.*, to the extent it prevented them from possessing, obtaining, or manufacturing cannabis for their personal medical use. A district court denied a motion for a preliminary injunction, but the United States Court of Appeals for the Ninth Circuit reversed.

Overview

Respondents were California residents who suffered from a variety of serious medical conditions and had sought to avail themselves of medical marijuana pursuant to the terms of the Compassionate Use Act, *Cal. Health & Safety Code § 11362.5* (2005). After an investigation, county officials concluded that one respondent's use of marijuana was entirely lawful under California law; nevertheless, federal agents seized and destroyed all six of her cannabis plants. The Court held that the regulation of marijuana under the CSA was squarely within Congress' commerce power because production of marijuana meant for home consumption had a substantial effect on supply and demand in the national market. Given the enforcement difficulties in distinguishing between marijuana cultivated locally and marijuana grown elsewhere, *21 U.S.C.S. § 801(5)*, and concerns about diversion into illicit channels, the Court had no difficulty concluding that Congress had a rational basis for believing that failure to regulate the intrastate manufacture and possession of marijuana would leave a gaping hole in the CSA. Congress was acting well within its authority of the Commerce Clause, U.S. Const., art. I, § 8.

Outcome
The judgment of the Court of Appeals was vacated. The case was remanded for further proceedings.

These are the Headnotes written by Lexis's editors. The number of headnotes can vary greatly. This case has been edited down from the original fifteen to the five that most closely match those made by West's editors.

(LexisNexis® Headnotes)

Criminal Law & Procedure > ... > Controlled Substances > Substance Schedules > General Overview

HN1 See *21 U.S.C.S. § 801(1)-(6)*.

Criminal Law & Procedure > ... > Controlled Substances > Manufacture > Elements

Criminal Law & Procedure > ... > Controlled Substances > Possession > General Overview

Criminal Law & Procedure > ... > Possession > Simple Possession > General Overview

Criminal Law & Procedure > ... > Possession > Simple Possession > Elements

Criminal Law & Procedure > ... > Controlled Substances > Substance Schedules > General Overview

HN3 In enacting the Controlled Substances Act (CSA), *21 U.S.C.S. § 801 et seq.*, Congress has classified marijuana as a Schedule I drug. *21 U.S.C.S. § 812(c)*.

Constitutional Law > Congressional Duties & Powers > Commerce Clause > General Overview

Constitutional Law > ... > Commerce Clause > Interstate Commerce > General Overview

Transportation Law > Interstate Commerce > Federal Powers

HN4 Congress has the power to regulate activities that substantially affect interstate commerce.

Constitutional Law > Congressional Duties & Powers > Commerce Clause > General Overview

Governments > Federal Government > US Congress

Transportation Law > Interstate Commerce > Federal Powers

Transportation Law > ... > Federal Powers > Powers of Congress > Substantial Relations

HN7 Congress' power to regulate commerce includes the power to prohibit commerce in a particular commodity.

Constitutional Law > Congressional Duties & Powers > Commerce Clause > General Overview

Governments > Federal Government > US Congress

HN10 Where the class of activities is regulated and that class is within the reach of federal power, the courts have no power to excise, as trivial, individual instances of the class.

Constitutional Law > Congressional Duties & Powers > Commerce Clause > General Overview

(Lawyers' Edition Display)

This section includes a summary and headnotes from Lawyer's Edition, an unofficial Reporter for the Supreme Court that was purchased by Lexis.

Decision

[***1] Controlled Substances Act's (*21 U.S.C.S. §§ 801 et seq.*) prohibition of marijuana manufacture and possession, as applied to intrastate manufacture and possession for medical purposes under California law, held not to exceed Congress' power under Federal Constitution's commerce clause (Art. I, § 8, cl. 3).

Summary

The federal Controlled Substances Act (CSA) (Title II of the Comprehensive Drug Abuse Prevention and Control Act) (*21 U.S.C.S. §§ 801 et seq.*) generally criminalized the manufacture, distribution, or possession of marijuana. Although marijuana sale or possession also was generally prohibited under California criminal law, California enacted in 1996 a statute that created an exemption from criminal prosecution for marijuana possession under state law for (1) physicians who recommended marijuana to patients for medical purposes; and (2) patients, and their primary caregivers, who possessed or cultivated marijuana for patients' personal medical purposes upon recommendation or approval by a physician.

[...]

Headnotes

COMMERCE §206 > -- marijuana -- local cultivation and use -- medicinal purposes -- state law > Headnote:

LEdHN[1A] [1A]*LEdHN[1B]* [1B]*LEdHN[1C]* [1C]*LEdHN[1D]* [1D]*LEdHN[1E]* [1E]*LEdHN[1F]* [1F]*LEdHN[1G]* [1G]

The categorical prohibition, under the Controlled Substances Act (CSA) (Title II of the Comprehensive Drug Abuse Prevention and Control Act) (*21 U.S.C.S. §§ 801 et seq.*), of the manufacture and possession of marijuana, did not-
-as applied to the intrastate manufacture and possession of marijuana for medical purposes pursuant to a state statute--exceed Congress' authority under the *Federal Constitution's commerce clause* (Art. I, § 8, cl. 3), as:

[...]

Syllabus

The Syllabus, written by the Reporter of Decisions at the U.S. Supreme Court begins here. We've edited this down, too.

California's Compassionate Use Act authorizes limited marijuana use for medicinal purposes. Respondents Raich and Monson are California residents who both use doctor-recommended marijuana for serious medical conditions. After federal Drug Enforcement Administration (DEA) agents seized and destroyed all six of Monson's cannabis plants, respondents brought this action seeking injunctive and declaratory relief prohibiting the enforcement of the federal Controlled Substances Act (CSA) to the extent it prevents them from possessing, obtaining, or manufacturing cannabis for their personal medical use. Respondents claim that enforcing the CSA against them would violate the *Commerce Clause* and other constitutional provisions. The District Court denied respondents' motion for a preliminary injunction, but the Ninth Circuit reversed, [***9] finding that they had demonstrated a strong likelihood of success on the claim that the CSA is an unconstitutional exercise of Congress' *Commerce Clause* authority as applied to the intrastate, noncommercial cultivation and possession of cannabis for personal medical purposes as recommended by a patient's physician pursuant to valid California state law. The court relied heavily on *United States v. Lopez, 514 U.S. 549, 131 L. Ed. 2d 626, 115 S. Ct. 1624,* and *United States v. Morrison, 529 U.S. 598, 146 L. Ed. 2d 658, 120 S. Ct. 1740,* to hold that this separate class of purely local activities was beyond the reach of federal power.

Held:

Congress' *Commerce Clause* authority includes the power to prohibit the local cultivation and use of marijuana in compliance with California law.

(a) For the purposes of consolidating various drug laws into a comprehensive statute, providing meaningful regulation over legitimate sources of drugs to prevent diversion into illegal channels, and strengthening law enforcement tools against international and interstate drug trafficking, Congress enacted the Comprehensive Drug Abuse Prevention and Control Act of 1970, Title II of which is the CSA. To effectuate the statutory goals, Congress devised a closed regulatory system making it unlawful to manufacture, distribute, dispense, or possess any controlled substance except as authorized by the CSA. *21 U.S.C. §§ 841(a)(1), 844(a).* All controlled substances are classified into five schedules, *§ 812,* based on their accepted medical uses, their potential for abuse, and their psychological and physical effects on the body, *§§ 811, 812.* Marijuana is classified as a Schedule I substance, *§ 812(c),* based on its high potential for abuse, no accepted medical use, and no accepted safety for use in medically supervised treatment, *§ 812(b)(1).* This classification renders the manufacture, distribution, or possession of marijuana a criminal offense. *§§ 841(a)(1), 844(a).*

(b) Congress' power to regulate purely local activities that are part of an economic "class of activities" that have a substantial effect on interstate commerce is firmly established. See, e.g., *Perez v. United States, 402 U.S. 146, 151, 28 L. Ed. 2d 686, 91 S. Ct. 1357.* If Congress decides that the "'total incidence'" of a practice poses a threat to a national market, it may regulate the entire class. See, e.g., *id., at 154-155, 28 L. Ed. 2d 686, 91 S. Ct. 1357.* Of particular relevance here is *Wickard v. Filburn, 317 U.S. 111, 127-128, 87 L. Ed. 122, 63 S. Ct. 82,* where, in rejecting the appellee farmer's contention that Congress' admitted power to regulate the production of wheat for commerce did not authorize federal regulation of wheat production intended wholly for the appellee's own consumption, the Court established that Congress can regulate purely intrastate activity that is not itself "commercial," *i.e.,* not produced for sale, if it concludes that failure to regulate that class of activity would undercut the regulation of the interstate market in that commodity. The similarities between this case and *Wickard* are striking. In both cases, the regulation is squarely within Congress' commerce power because production of the commodity meant for home consumption, be it wheat or marijuana, has a substantial effect on supply and demand in the national market for that commodity. **[***10]** In assessing the scope of Congress' *Commerce Clause* authority, the Court need not determine whether respondents' activities, taken in the aggregate, substantially affect interstate commerce in fact, but only whether a "rational basis" exists for so concluding. *E.g., Lopez, 514 U.S., at 557, 131 L. Ed. 2d 626, 115 S. Ct. 1624.* Given the enforcement difficulties that attend distinguishing between marijuana cultivated locally and marijuana grown elsewhere, *21 U.S.C. § 801(5),* and concerns about diversion into illicit channels, the Court has no difficulty concluding that Congress had a rational basis for believing that failure to regulate the intrastate manufacture and possession of marijuana would leave a gaping hole in the CSA.

(c) Respondents' heavy reliance on *Lopez* and *Morrison* overlooks the larger context of modern-era *Commerce Clause* jurisprudence preserved by those cases, while also reading those cases far too broadly. The statutory challenges at issue there were markedly different from the challenge here. Respondents ask the Court to excise individual applications of a concededly valid comprehensive statutory scheme. In contrast, in both *Lopez* and *Morrison,* the parties asserted that a particular statute or provision fell outside Congress' commerce power in its entirety. This distinction is pivotal for the Court has often reiterated that '[w]here the class of activities is regulated and that class is within the reach of federal power, the courts have no power 'to excise, as trivial, individual instances' of the class." *Perez, 402 U.S., at 154, 28 L. Ed. 2d 686, 91 S. Ct. 1357.* Moreover, the Court emphasized that the laws at issue in *Lopez* and *Morrison* had nothing to do with "commerce" or any sort of economic enterprise. See *Lopez, 514 U.S., at 561, 131 L. Ed. 2d 626, 115 S. Ct. 1624; Morrison, 529 U.S., at 610, 146 L. Ed. 2d 658, 120 S. Ct. 1740.* In contrast, the CSA regulates quintessentially economic activities: the production, distribution, and consumption of commodities for which there is an established, and lucrative, interstate market. Prohibiting the intrastate possession or manufacture of an article of commerce is a rational means of regulating commerce in that product. The Ninth Circuit cast doubt on the CSA's constitutionality by isolating a distinct class of activities that it held to be beyond the reach of federal power: the intrastate, noncommercial cultivation, possession, and use of marijuana for personal medical purposes on the advice of a physician and in accordance with state law. However, Congress clearly acted rationally in determining that this subdivided class of activities is an essential part of the larger regulatory scheme. The case comes down to the claim that a locally cultivated product that is used domestically rather than sold on the open market is not subject to federal regulation. Given the CSA's findings and the undisputed magnitude of the commercial market for marijuana, *Wickard* and its progeny foreclose that claim.

352 F.3d 1222, vacated and remanded.

Counsel: Paul D. Clement argued the cause for petitioners.

Randy E. Barnett argued the cause for respondents.

Name of Counsel

Judges: Stevens, J., delivered the opinion of the Court, in which Kennedy, Souter, Ginsburg, and Breyer, JJ., joined. Scalia, J., filed an opinion concurring in the judgment. O'Connor, J., filed a dissenting opinion, **[***11]** in which Rehnquist, C. J., and Thomas, J., joined as to all but Part III. Thomas, J., filed a dissenting opinion.

Opinion by: STEVENS

Opinion | The opinion begins here.

[*5] [**2198] Justice **Stevens** delivered the opinion of the Court.

LEdHN California is one of at least nine States that authorize the use of marijuana for medicinal purposes. [1] The question presented [**2199] in this case is whether the power vested in Congress by Article I, § 8, of the Constitution "[t]o make all Laws which shall be necessary and proper for carrying into Execution" its authority to "regulate Commerce with foreign Nations, and among the several States" includes the power to prohibit the local cultivation and use of marijuana in compliance with California law.

CHAPTER 3

CASE FINDING

There are millions of cases out there. No kidding, there are millions of them. Each year more than one hundred thousand new ones are added to the mix. There is a good side to this and a bad side. The good side is that somewhere out there in the trackless swamp of judicial opinions there may be one that helps you. The bad side is that you have to figure out how you can possibly find it. You will not be surprised to learn that there are a variety of ways to accomplish this feat. These are:

- The Truly Excellent Method
- Algorithmic Searching
- Terms and Connectors Searching
- Subject Systems
- Citation Chasing
- Secondary Sources
- Annotated Codes

We will look at them in order. The surprise ending to this chapter will be a sobering conclusion. No peeking ahead.

I. THE TRULY EXCELLENT METHOD

The truly excellent method of case finding is to start with a good case in hand. Once you have one good case you can leverage it into a lot of information. You can take the citation to that case to almost any legal tool (such as Lexis and Westlaw) and you will be plugged into a research system. Most of the research systems are organized around cases. Having one good case in hand will give you the "hook" that you need to tap into them.

Leave it to us to say that the best way to find cases is to start with a case. What good is that to you? Actually, it is a good tip. You often will start a research problem with a case from your casebook or from your moot court assignment. If you are in the real world, the person who is giving you the research assignment might be the best source for you. There may be materials that come along with the research problem such as filings, briefs or previous work product that give you relevant cases. The assigning attorney just might say, "Here are a few good cases." If she doesn't, ask if she has suggestions. One of the realities of legal research is that a knowledgeable human being can save you time.

If you cannot find a human being, use some of the contextual tools discussed in Chapter 1. Never embark on research in a database as large as the universe of cases without knowing as much as you can about the topic which you are searching. Do not start with a case, start by getting background.

II. ALGORITHMIC SEARCHING

a. Overview of Algorithmic Searching

Westlaw and Lexis have moved to a new generation of searching which doesn't require you to use arcane search commands to formulate a query. The early iterations of this type of searching was marketed by Westlaw and Lexis as "natural language." We will still discuss terms and connectors in the next section but that is no longer the default method of searching for most users.

So what is this algorithmic searching? For all of us, Google has become the search engine of choice, and while Google offers plenty of advanced searching techniques, the default mode of searching is to type words into the query box. The same is true of Westlaw and Lexis. Essentially, you just type in any old sentence into the big blue (Westlaw) or red (Lexis) search box, and the underlying search algorithms developed by the very smart computer scientists will parse your search, recognize what you really want and run your search. The algorithms that drive these systems are proprietary and contain major secrets but we do know that they do some pretty fancy work such as weighting the relevance of your terms, locating synonyms and word variations, identifying legal concepts and phrases, using citation analysis to see how much a particular case has been cited and analyzing usage patterns of other users, Importantly, they also leverage the significant editorial work that has gone into producing the headnotes and key numbers by bringing back cases that are classified into those mighty subject systems (again more on that below.)

Some who teach legal research don't like the algorithmic searching because it feels sloppy, whereas traditional terms and connectors searches call for precise thought and careful planning. Algorithmic searching seems less rigorous and requires the user to trust the underlying search algorithm which is opaque to the searcher. However, the train has already left the station and while terms and connectors searching still has its place in the sophisticated users toolbox, most users are going to put their trust in the smart computer scientists and the ever adapting algorithms.

b. Strategies for Algorithmic Searching

Do not try to psych out the search algorithm, or write a grammatically correct sentence. The machine does not care. Put in what you think the relevant terms are and let the computer do the work. If you put in too many terms, especially ones that are uncommon, it may induce the systems to give too much weight to those unusual terms, throwing off your results. On the other hand putting in too few terms, especially if they are common terms, doesn't give the system enough information to work it's magic. You are trying to find the golden mean.

You can always try searching from the main screens of Westlaw and Lexis and then using the filtering options that present themselves after the search has been completed to narrow down your results. However, we feel that you are better served if you actually spend a little time doing four things.

1. Limit your search to cases (presuming you are doing case research). Both Westlaw and Lexis allow you to browse to cases and then search from there. A golden rule of all searching is to search the smallest database possible. But before you do that you should move on to tip #2.

2. Limit by jurisdiction and date. If you have a research problem that is in California, then after you have followed tip #1, you would choose to search cases by state—in this instance, California. You may also want to limit by date as well. This can be especially true if you are familiar with an area of the law up

until a certain point in time and just want to see more recent cases.

3.   For those of you who want to get really sophisticated, you can search for cases in a specific practice area. Rather than limiting by jurisdiction (tip #2) you can choose to limit to cases in a particular topic. Of course, this requires you to know a little about legal issues presented in the research problem and to choose the appropriate practice area. This just might not be possible, especially as a newly minted 1L. In that case, you can go back to tip #2.

4.   Look past the top five cases in your search results (but don't go down to result number 100.) You will always get some results back regardless of your search terms. However, Westlaw and Lexis live and die by the efficacy of the search algorithms. The results will come back, by default, in order of relevance. Experience tells us that if you don't see results that seem relevant to the user in the top 30, then it is time to tweak your search.

III.   TERMS AND CONNECTORS SEARCHING

Terms and connectors searching (also known as Boolean searching) allows you to search on Westlaw or Lexis for specific words and phrases in your target database. By using "and," "or" and proximity connectors (the ones which find words close to one another) you can ask the system to retrieve documents that contain only those words for you. Until the advent of algorithmic searching this was the way everyone searched Westlaw or Lexis, and we still believe that terms and connectors has a place in the legal researcher's bag of tricks. In any case, we cannot tell you how to do it here. That would be like telling you how to ride a bicycle by having you read a set of written directions. Terms and connectors searching is one of those things that you have to do in order to understand. But we can offer the following advice.

Take the training that Lexis and Westlaw offer you and if they don't cover terms and connectors searching ask them about it. There are differences between the systems and there are subtleties that are worth knowing. Would we lie to you about this? Do not rely on your admittedly brilliant intuition to help you construct your search. Remember, the systems will always kick back an answer. The quality of the answer that you will get depends on the quality of your query and the ability to understand and manipulate the different connectors.

Algorithmic searching has relegated terms and connectors to the second tier of both Westlaw and Lexis. On both systems you will need to dig around to find it. Generally, it is to be found under "advanced" search or searching. Those advanced pages will provide many search options including a quick cheat sheet of the most common connectors used on the systems.

Even more important, lean in closer now, is the following: Are you listening? YOU ARE NOT AS GOOD A TERMS AND CONNECTORS SEARCHER AS YOU THINK THAT YOU ARE! All the studies show that in large databases no one is a very good terms and connector searcher. The language that judges use in writing opinions is just too imprecise. If a judge is writing an opinion that involves a child she might refer to that child as a child, a minor, an infant, a dependent, a boy, or Skippy because that is his name. Judges are by nature idiosyncratic creatures who get to say whatever they want. If the language used is eccentric enough, only a mind reader will be able to draw up a terms and connector search that pulls up the most relevant case. Does this mean that you should despair? No. Here are some of our tips about terms and connectors searching.

1.   Know a good deal about your search. You should factor in buzz words and terms of art, use hooks such as the names of cases, statutes and regulations.

2.   Go back to the tips on algorithmic searching and follow them:

Use the smallest database possible

Limit by jurisdiction and date, especially if you just want more recent cases

If possible, limit by topic or practice area

Look at the cases below the top five, but not much past result 30

3.   Use document fields or segments to limit your search. Your Westlaw and Lexis trainers will show you how to use

segment and field searches that will have the effect of shrinking the database for your search. Keep in mind that every time you enter a search on Westlaw or Lexis you can create your own subset of cases to be searched.

The typical human wants to jump in to searching as soon as possible. The front-ends of Westlaw and Lexis are so good that you can start using them without any help. But if you do that you run the risk of being one of those sad souls who wanders into the swamp and never comes back. Yes, you will get answers but they will be reckless and we know you are not like that. Heed our plaintive cries.

IV. SUBJECT SYSTEMS

a. West's Topics and Key Numbers: The American Digest System

When legal research was done exclusively in books the world of available cases was defined by the National Reporter System, that lovely mastodon described earlier. West was reporting every case that made it into print and preparing a headnote for each point of law that was determined in each case. It did not stop there. Beginning at the end of the 19th Century West adopted a system for classifying law called the American Digest System. Designed by a genius named John Mallory, this system broke all of American law into a series of topics. Within each top level topic there were as many subdivisions as necessary to fully sketch out the area of law. The subdivisions were called Key Numbers, and the whole thing came to be known as the Topic and Key Number System.

For each case that West was publishing in the National Reporter system an editor prepared a headnote for each point of law decided in that case. It was thus possible to take each headnote of each case and place it in its pre-defined location in the Topic and Key number system. Thus West developed a huge reservoir of headnotes for all published decisions, sorted by Topic and Key Number. The collected headnotes were published in huge sets of volumes called digests, organized in Topic and Key Number order for each state and for the federal courts.

The essential point to grasp is that if you knew the Topic and Key Number that covered a topic that you were researching, you had a powerful entry point into an enormous, and enormously sophisticated, classification system.

Bob loves the American Digest System and the intellectual chutzpah that went into its creation. There is a real beauty to the system. Many lawyers who went to law school before the digital age tend to think in the categories of the Topic and Key Number system. Even if they never really understood how it worked, it was the only game in town. They learned it by osmosis.

These days a researcher will most likely use the Topic and Key Number as a hidden but essential part of the algorithmic searching on Westlaw. It won't be obvious to you but your search terms are also querying the Topic, Key Numbers and headnotes that are an integral part of the West system. You are taking advantage of this mighty subject system without even knowing it.

There is however, a simple way of using the Topic and Key Number system and it harkens back to the Truly Excellent Method discussed earlier in this chapter. Once you have found one or two good cases you can leverage the Topic and Key Number system within those cases to find other cases that discuss the same point of law. For example, in *Gonzales v. Raich,* if you are interested in the Commerce Clause and the power to regulate local activities you can use the headnote that classified to Topic 83 (Commerce) and Key Number 7(2) (Activities Affecting Interstate Commerce). This might seem complicated but all you have to do is look at the headnotes in the *Raich* case and click on the handy link to that Topic and Key Number (see the screenshot below)

2	Commerce		
	Commerce Clause grants Congress power to regulate purely local activities that are part of economic class of activities that have substantial effect on interstate commerce. U.S.C.A. Const. Art. 1, § 8, cl. 3.	83	Commerce
		83I	Power to Regulate in General
		83k2	Constitutional Grant of Power to Congress
	355 Cases that cite this headnote	83k7	Internal Commerce of States
		83k7(2)	Activities Affecting Interstate Commerce

By doing that you have created your own mini-database of other cases that discuss the same point of law about "activities affecting interstate commerce." At this point you can go further and change your jurisdiction to meet your specific research needs. In the screen shot below we have created our own mini-database of cases that:

- Contains cases discussing the "activities affecting interstate commerce."

- Contains cases from California state and federal courts, and the US Supreme Court

(2) Activities affecting interstate commerce (94) ⓘ

Jurisdiction: California (State & Fed.), United States Supreme Court   Change

---

1 - 94   Sort by: Topic then Date   ▾

☐ Select all items   No items selected

---

    83 COMMERCE (Up to 10,000)
    — 83I Power to Regulate in General 1,803
    ——— 83⇔2 Constitutional Grant of Power to Congress 1,048
    ————— 83⇔7 Internal Commerce of States 167
    ——————— 83⇔7(2) Activities affecting interstate commerce. 132

So to briefly recap, you have leveraged the massive Topic and Key Number system to find other like cases in your particular jurisdiction and all done with just a few clicks of your mouse.

b.   Lexis Subject System

Lexis also has a classification system for its cases, allowing the researcher to again use the Truly Excellent Method in combination with a comprehensive system of case classification. Unlike Westlaw, the system on Lexis has never existed in the paper universe and they also don't use a numerical system like the Topic and Key Numbers.

Taking *Gonzales v. Raich*, you can leverage the headnotes created by Lexis to find others cases on a similar point of law. In this case on Lexis, Headnote #5 covers similar ground to the headnote we used above in Westlaw on the power of Congress to regulate activities affecting interstate commerce—see the screenshot below of Headnote #5 from the case on Lexis.

Constitutional Law > Congressional Duties & Powers ▾ > 📄 Commerce Clause ▾ > General Overview ▾
Governments > Federal Government ▾ > US Congress ▾
Transportation Law > Interstate Commerce ▾ > Federal Powers ▾
Transportation Law > ... > Federal Powers ▾ > Powers of Congress ▾ > Substantial Relations ▾

HN5 ⚖ United States Supreme Court case law firmly establishes Congress' power to regulate purely local activities that are part of an economic class of activities that have a substantial effect on interstate commerce. Even if a person's activity be local and though it may not be regarded as commerce, it may still, whatever its nature, be reached by Congress if it exerts a substantial economic effect on interstate commerce. The Supreme Court has never required Congress to legislate with scientific exactitude. When Congress decides that the total incidence of a practice poses a threat to a national market, it may regulate the entire class. In this vein, the Supreme Court has reiterated that when a general regulatory statute bears a substantial relation to commerce, the de minimis character of individual instances arising under that statute is of no consequence. *Shepardize - Narrow by this Headnote*

The researcher can then use the breadcrumb trail to find other cases, that for example, have been placed in the category:

Constitutional Law > Congressional Duties & Powers > Commerce Clause > General Overview

There is the ability on subsequent screens to further narrow the database of results to only include jurisdictions of interest. While the mechanics of the process are slightly different on Lexis than Westlaw, the underlying research strategy is the same—take your few cases and leverage them using the headnotes.

V. OTHER CASE FINDING SERVICES

In the ever developing world of legal research services, there are new players of widely varying sizes entering the marketplace. On the behemoth end of the scale is Bloomberg Law (http://www.bloomberglaw.com), which is an outgrowth of the Bloomberg business and news information company. Bloomberg Law provides access to case law from all jurisdictions in the United States as well a wide range of secondary materials. Many law schools are providing students with passwords to Bloomberg Law along with Lexis and Westlaw.

On a smaller scale there lower cost services such as Casemaker (http://www.casemaker.us), and Fastcase (http://www.fastcase.com). Ravel Law (http://www. ravellaw.com) is free for law students and attempts to present cases and the interrelationship between cases in a more visual format than other services. Then there are more open public legal resources, for example Casetext (https://casetext.com/). There is a good deal of flux in the market for legal information and while it might not affect you in your first year of law school, it is worth keeping in mind as you progress through law school.

VI. CITATION CHASING

We devote a separate chapter to the use of citation systems so we are not going into them in any depth here. You should also check out the video on citators that accompany this book. We would be remiss, however, if we did not point out that many researchers use citators such as Shepard's or KeyCite to find cases. Once you have a case that discusses your point of law you can use that case to see other cases that cite your case. They may well be talking about the same issue. Lots of interesting research is being done on using citation clustering as a search engine. Even if you do not know a peanut butter cluster from a citation cluster, you will be using these systems.

VII.   ANNOTATED CODES

In the chapter where we discuss statutory materials we will praise annotated codes, but just as with citators, we have to mention them here and remind you of the video on legislation that discusses annotated codes. Frequently in real life and occasionally in law school, your research problem will begin with or contain a statute. The relevant annotated code section will collect all the cases that mention that statute for you. Annotated codes are great case catchers. This makes annotated codes great places to find that one good case that we have talked about, or if you already have a good case that cites to a statute, the annotated code will lead you to other relevant cases.

For example, in *Gonzales v. Raich*, the opinion discusses and cites 21 USC 801, a section of the *Controlled Substances Act*. By looking at 21 USC 801 on Westlaw or Lexis you will be able to see the cases that have mentioned the statute. On Westlaw they are called "Notes of Decisions" and on Lexis, "Case Notes."

VIII.   SECONDARY SOURCES

In Chapter 1 we discussed the array of sources that you might encounter in the first year of law school and Bob discussed them in the video on secondary sources. We stressed using some of those tools to get a feel for the context of your research problem. Those sources work for finding cases by subject. Hornbooks, nutshells, even outlines can lead you to a relevant case.

Law reviews can also be good places to find cases, but in your first semester of law school they will not play a major role. They can, however, be useful tools if you find a law review article that deals with your case in some detail. If you want a detailed treatment on using law reviews, check one of the longer research books.

Circling briefly, back to citators for moment. We mentioned that citators (Shepards and KeyCite) are great places for finding cases that cite your case. You can also use the citator to find secondary sources that cite your case. You can then use that secondary source to find discussion of your issue of law with analysis of relevant cases. We are in sense moving in a circle—a good case to a citator to a relevant secondary source to more good cases.

A Sobering Conclusion

When you arrive at law school you will be operating in a new world. New terms will abound and lots of your classmates will appear to be much smarter than you are. You will want to prove yourself. You will be anxious. When you are given a research problem you will wish to leap into it. Often you will think that the answer to your research task will be to find a case. Filled with nervous energy you will want to plunge into legal research databases to find a case. If we had a dime for every first year law student who has asked us a question like, "I tried to find out about the First Amendment as is applies to high school students, where can I find a case?" We would not be rich but we would certainly have a lot dimes.

Frequently the worst place to start your research is to go looking for a case. Get some context first. Discover the parameters of the problems. Know your turf. Then you can go read cases. We know that it is tempting to leap in. There are these great search systems for cases, Westlaw and Lexis, that lie there shimmering just inches away. And no matter what search terms you enter you will get results. But please, for our sake, don't jump into that roiling ocean of contradictory precedent

until you have background. We feel compelled to say this at the
end of the chapter on case finding. It's just the way we are. We
leave you with a few Quick Tips.

Quick Tips for Case Finding

Before you start your online research, sit down with a pencil
(and possibly a dictionary) and think about the words that
describe your issue. English is a rich, complex, synonym-filled
language and judges use all manner of word combinations. If you
want to find the cases they wrote, so should you.

Use the smallest database you can for your search and
eliminate some false hits. Why search cases from the federal
court when you're researching a state issue? Why search
insurance cases when you're researching a family law issue?

Consider not going the online route first. Is there a treatise
on your topic? Treatises have lovely indices and lots of case
citations which can help you, in addition to some plain talk (well,
as plain as lawyers ever get) about the issues. Most, but not all,
are available online, although experience tells us that oftentimes
the print version are easier to use when you are getting started
on a topic. Don't know if there is a treatise on your topic? Ask for
help from those friendly librarians at the reference desk, they'll
help you find one, or make other suggestions. They may even
have a handy research guide available on their website for just
this purpose.

CHAPTER 4

USING CITATORS

Citators are the lynchpin of legal research both academically and professionally. Excuse us if we've shocked you with such a serious statement, but citators deserve to be taken seriously—someday, they will save you from certain humiliation.

- First, a little bit about citators.

- Next, we'll describe what they'll do for you.

- Last, we'll talk a bit about how they can improve your life.

I. A SHORT HISTORY OF CITATORS

The law is constantly changing. Legislatures are meeting, and judges and their clerks are churning out decisions even as you read this. At some point in your legal career, you will probably find the "perfect" case—the one that directly answers the question your supervising partner, (whom you would so like to impress), asked. Before you take this beautiful case to that partner, you must ask yourself: is this case still good law? As the case moved through the court system did a higher court overrule it? As time passed has the same court reversed itself? The partner might ask if the case you found has been influential? Has it gained adherents for its view? Or have a series of subsequent decisions, while not overruling or reversing it, criticized it so sharply that it would be a liability if it was cited? If you can't answer these questions for that partner, you risk embarrassment and possibly, given the wrong circumstances, unemployment. If you can't answer such questions for a judge, you risk more severe penalties.[1] Lawyers need tools to monitor

---

[1] Rule 11 of the Federal Rules of Civil Procedure, for example, requires an attorney to only present, " . . . claims, defenses, and other legal contentions . . . warranted by existing law or by a nonfrivolous argument for the extension, modification, or reversal of existing law or the establishment of new law." The rule allows for sanctions against an attorney who doesn't. Now you know why we take this section so seriously—as your Mother might have said, it's for your own good. Read the whole rule and commentary at: https://www.law.cornell.edu/rules/frcp.

the life of cases and to keep track of a case as it moves through time.

For 120 years, this function was performed almost exclusively by an ingenious, wonderfully obsessive-compulsive, research tool called *Shepard's Citations*. In 1873, Frank Shepard began printing lists of citations to Illinois Supreme Court cases on gummed paper for attorneys to stick in the margins of their bound reporters. Before long he began publishing his citation lists in book form, and coverage expanded gradually to include every state and the federal courts. The idea of using one of the Shepard's citators to check up on a case became so much a part of the fabric of the practice of law that lawyers gave the ultimate compliment to Frank Shepard, and his name became a verb. Each day thousands of lawyers are asked "to shepardize" a case. Indeed, learning to use the volumes of Shepard's became one of the great hazing experiences of American law school. Luckily you will almost certainly never use the paper version of Shepard's.

Until 1997 the Shepard's company occupied a unique place in legal research—there was no competition. Shepard's citators remained a neutral source used by everyone. Courts required all attorneys to "shepardize." You may wonder how the entire legal profession came to rely on the products of one publisher for such a vital function. Even more amazing, the acceptance was uncritical. Shepard's citators simply WERE the world of citation.[2]

After a century of peace in the world of citators, the end of the 20th Century saw very big changes. In 1997 Reed Elsevier, the company which owns Lexis, purchased the Shepard's company. This put Shepard's citators directly in the camp of one of the two competing full-text online systems. Reed Elsevier also announced that at the end of its current licensing agreement with the West Group, it would no longer allow Shepard's to appear on Westlaw. Shepard's citators were no longer neutral. If only the Lexis system had the universally used citator, imagine the effect on legal research—especially for Westlaw.

---

[2] We don't have an explanation, except to say that Shepard's was doing a good job, and if you take a look at one of the paper volumes you might understand why no one else wanted to do it.

Foreseeing such a grim scenario, in 1997 West Group introduced *KeyCite*, the first product to truly compete with Shepard's. KeyCite is an online (only) citating system. KeyCite performs the verification functions of Shepard's as well as supplying the same opportunities for expanding your research. Despite concerns by older researchers that it would have serious trouble getting accepted by the legal world the market took to KeyCite right away. Since 1999 there has been keen competition between the two systems, and that has been a good thing for legal research since both systems have improved tremendously since that time. It is also a bad thing for legal research as now there are two places to go, and they sometimes do not tell you the same information. While you are in law school you will have the opportunity to use each of them. Take advantage and use the comparative shopping technique.

In this Chapter we will describe each system and tell you what you'll be using them for. The online versions change their look so rapidly that if we try to write down exactly how to point and click your way through the systems we'll immediately be woefully out of date. For the mechanics, you should rely on your instructors and the Westlaw and Lexis trainers. We won't provide a description of how to use the paper version of Shepard's either as you are now very unlikely to experience the joys of shepardizing in this old fashioned way.

II. WHAT CITATORS ACTUALLY DO FOR YOU

a. The Three Functions of Citators

Citators perform three basic functions. The first is *verification of authority*. The citator tells you if your case is still good law by noting whether or not it has been overruled or reversed.

The second function is to tell you *how the case been treated by other courts* in their opinions. Have subsequent courts cited it favorably, criticized or ignored it? Judicial decisions are organic. Their precedential value can go up or down. Subsequent cases may cite it a lot, or they may criticize or limit it. This kind of treatment can make your case stronger or weaker.

Citators play a third function by *pointing you to potential research sources*. The theory runs like this: if a subsequent case cites your case, even if it does not affect the validity or strength of your case, it must be discussing some of the same issues. Citation chasing is a popular research strategy, and often works well. In fact, citators point to secondary materials beyond cases.

The driving principle of the Shepard's and KeyCite citators is very straightforward. Using the same obsessive approach that John West employed in creating the National Reporter System, Frank Shepard determined that his system would allow the researcher to see every subsequent mention of a case. Let me repeat that: *every subsequent mention of a case*.[3] This catches any important comments on a case, but it also catches every trivial mention as well. It is up to you to sift through it, although both systems have sophisticated filtering mechanisms to help you do this efficiently.

b. Coverage

Shepard's and KeyCite's coverage of cases is fully retrospective in the online systems—that's back into the 1700s. Additionally, both systems include the unpublished opinions that appear online. Non-case materials in both systems include as citing references a dizzying array of secondary legal materials that help you understand and interpret cases and points of law.

The citators are updated on a daily basis, which means that approximately twenty-four to forty-eight hours after Lexis and Westlaw receive a case, it has been incorporated as a cited (and a citing) reference.

---

[3] Every subsequent mention of a case. This is worth pondering. Do you know how many times other courts have cited *Roe v. Wade*? If you'd really like to know, Shepard's or KeyCite can tell you.

III. WHAT YOU GET WHEN YOU SHEPARDIZE OR KEYCITE A CASE

a. Parallel Citations

Citators provide one of the easiest ways to find parallel citations. No matter what citation is typed in, the information retrieved will include a list that has the official and any other unofficial citations to the cited case. If you have to update the case, this is an efficient way to find all the parallel cites.

b. A Quick Word About Nomenclature

When we discuss citators we often refer to the "cited" case and "citing" cases or references. Take the example of *Gonzales v. Raich*. When you s=Shepardize or Keycite Gonzales, that becomes the "cited" case. The various subsequent cases, statutes, and secondary sources that have cited Gonzales are the "citing" cases or references. Just keep this in mind as we discuss the other features of citators.

c. History: The Ones Which Can Reverse or Affirm Your Case

Appellate History (in Shepard's) or History (in KeyCite) citations, i.e., those indicating prior or subsequent proceedings in the same case, are features in both citators. The most significant history citations for determining a case's validity are subsequent decisions by a higher appellate court in the same jurisdiction.[4] The citation to the higher court's decision always indicates if the cited case is affirmed, modified, or reversed on appeal.

The history notations are the first step in determining whether or not the case being checked is still good law. If a case was reversed on appeal, you cannot cite it *as authority*. Our italics seem to imply there might be reasons for you to cite a case that has been reversed by a higher court, don't they? Even if your case was reversed, there may be sections worth reading or

---

[4] This issue of jurisdiction is a big deal. You will learn about it in Civil Procedure. A case from the California Supreme Court might be of interest to a court in New Mexico, but it is not authoritative. Of course it matters a lot to a court in California.

reasoning worth considering. Such a case *can* be cited as long as it is clearly noted that it is not binding precedent.

It is even possible that a higher court decision is listed as "reversed" because of a separate issue in your case—not the one you're researching—and your case will still be good law on your issue. The only way to know is by finding the spot where the citing case uses your case and analyzing how your case has been used. The language notations in a citat that assist in case analysis are no substitute for reading the decisions themselves. The first clue as to what has happened to a case in either Shepard's or KeyCite is a red or yellow signal. Red means the editors have decided there has been some definite sort of negative history, yellow means there may be. Remember, these are just clues, and should alert you to look carefully, not to use them in place of your own analysis. You will be staking your client's claim on your own analysis.

While only those decisions which directly affect the result in your case are considered part of its history, a decision need not be reversed or modified by a higher court to have its status as authority diminished or erased. Subsequent unrelated decisions, by overruling the case or limiting its holding, may yet have an important impact on its status as precedent. As part of the initial display, KeyCite attempts to ferret out these cases under the heading "Negative Indirect History" within the overall "Negative Treatment" tab within KeyCite.

d.   Treatment and Related Cases, the Ones Which Can Erode or Bolster Your Case

Running your case through one of the citators often yields a list of subsequent citing references to cases that have cited your case. In a Shepard's display, these are called "citing decisions" and in KeyCite "citing references." To display just citing cases with KeyCite, you must filter by cases from within the "citing references" tab. (At this point, it's probably a good idea for you to know that there are a few screenshots of both KeyCite and Shepard's at the end of this chapter—you can see much of what we're describing on those screen shots.)

Both citators provide several clues to the attitudes expressed by later courts about your case. The treatment of a

case by later decisions may have just as important an effect on
its precedential value as a direct reversal or affirmance. Courts
do not like to reverse themselves for a variety of reasons, so they
seek other means to weaken a precedent by limiting its
application to very restricted circumstances. Or a lower court
that is faced with a distasteful decision from a higher court may
seek to maneuver around it, distinguishing it from the case at
hand by one fact or another. These are the same analytical tricks
that will be on display in the classroom as your professor makes
you and your classmates compare cases. Such treatment can kill
the power of a precedent with a thousand small cuts. You need
to know.

Over the decades Shepard's has developed an editorial
system for indicating if the citing reference had a specific effect
upon the cited case. Within Shepard's you will see this analysis
of citing cases by entries such as "Distinguished by", "Criticized
by", or "Followed by." There are a good number of these "editorial
phrases" that could possibly be assigned to the citing cases by
the editors at Lexis and it is aimed to assist you in
understanding the subsequent treatment of the cited case. In
addition, Lexis has a "depth of discussion" feature—from one to
four bars—telling you whether your citing case has analyzed,
discussed, mentioned or merely cited your case.

KeyCite has very similar features to Shepard's as the two
citators have each added functionality over the years in an
attempt to keep pace with each other. KeyCite was originally
designed to point to how much discussion of your case is
contained in the citing case. A system of bars, from one to four,
tells you the extent of the treatment of your case. There is also
now an editorial description of citing cases with terminology
such as "Distinguished by," "Declined to Extend by" and
"Examined by" and oversized quotation marks tell you whether
language from your case is quoted.

In the appellate history or history sections of Shepard's and
KeyCite, the references are to the first page of the relevant case.
In citing decisions or citing references, on the other hand, a
reference to the exact page within a decision on which your case
is cited is given in addition to the first page. These "pin-point" or

"pin-cite" page references allow you to jump to the exact place in the opinion where the case is being discussed.

Some of the citations are assigned words or phrases to indicate the attitude or effect of the subsequent decisions, such as "Distinguished by" which we mentioned above. It is important to note that in assigning these notations, the specific language of the court is largely relied upon. Shepard's editors have, in particular, developed a reputation for being conservative, and hence they will not indicate that a case has been overruled if such effect is not expressly stated in the later decision, no matter how contrary the holding.[5] This is one reason why the citator had such universal acceptance for so long. Don't forget: other indicators, such as "Criticized by" or "Limited by " may be just as important as an "Overruled by" in determining the value of a decision's precedent.[6]

The citations in the citing decisions or citing references sections of Shepard's and KeyCite listings can be sorted and filtered in numerous ways. A logical first sort on Shepard's is by court from highest to lowest, with decisions from the same jurisdiction as the cited case listed first and then ordered chronologically. *There is no ranking by importance or effect*

---

[5]   In perhaps the most famous instance, for over thirty years, *Shepard's United States Citations* indicated that the separate-but-equal doctrine of *Plessy v. Ferguson,* 163 U.S. 537 (1896), was **questioned** in *Brown v. Board of Education,* 347 U.S. 483 (1954), rather than **overruled** by *Brown.* Only when Judge John R. Brown noted this fact in a relatively recent opinion, *United States v. Holmes,* 822 F.2d 481, 503 n.2 (5th Cir. 1987) (Brown, J., concurring and dissenting), did Shepard's add a belated "overruled" notation in its *Plessy* entry. Although Shepard's follows the express words of opinions, it can occasionally be swayed by later criticism.

[6]   In *Glassalum Engineering Corp. v. 392208 Ontario Ltd.,* 487 So.2d 87 (Fla.App. 1986), the appellee relied on a case, *Gonzalez v. Ryder Systems, Inc.,* 327 So.2d 826 (Fla.App. 1976), the holding of which had been abrogated by an amendment to the Florida Rules of Civil Procedure. As the court noted:

By Sheparizing the *Gonzalez* case, one would have been alerted that its soundness or reasoning had been questioned in a later case; and by reading that later case, *Rivera v. A.M.I.F., Inc.,* 417 So.2d 304, one would have discovered that *Gonzalez* is no longer the law. . . .

If counsel did not observe Shepard's "questioned" signal (designated by a "q") and read *Rivera,* then they, at the least, performed inadequately: appellant's counsel (now the beneficiary of this court's own research) lost the opportunity to argue the controlling *Rivera* case; appellee's counsel, the opportunity to attempt to convince this court why we should not, as we do, find *Rivera* dispositive. Without belaboring the point, we remind the bar that, as this case so dramatically shows, cases must be Sheparized and that when Sheparizing, counsel must mind the "p's" and "q's." 487 So.2d at 88 (footnotes omitted).

on the cited case. A citation to an overruling case may appear towards the end of a long list of other cases. Depending on the jurisdiction of the case you are researching, citing references in federal cases and decisions from other jurisdictions follow the list of citations from your case's jurisdiction.

Using KeyCite the most obvious initial sort is by depth of treatment a court gives to the cited case (highest first.) A court that "examined" the cited case will have extended discussion of the cited case; "discussed" is substantial discussion; "cited" is some discussion and "mentioned" is a brief reference. As a visual clue, KeyCite assigns bars to reflect the amount of discussion within the citing references, i.e., an "examined" case gets four bars, a "discussed" case gets three, and so on. KeyCite indicates if the citing reference directly quotes the case being researched by placing quotation marks next to the citing reference. A direct quotation of a decision can be a powerful thing.

Beyond these more basic ways of sorting citing decisions, both Shepard's and KeyCite allow you to filter or narrow by numerous parameters. On Shepard's you could narrow the citing references to the *Raich* case by Analysis (for example, all citing cases that are notated "Distinguished by" or "Criticized by"), and are in the 9th Circuit and California State Courts. Likewise in KeyCite you could narrow by jurisdiction (for example, 9th Circuit Court of Appeals, California Federal District and California State Courts), combined with depth of treatment of four and three bars.

Shepard's and KeyCite each employ another notation system to aid you when you are interested in a particular point of law. Citing references indicate the headnote number of your case that corresponds to the specific issue being discussed. If a case addresses several issues but only one aspect is relevant to a particular research problem, one simply determines which headnote addresses the issue and scans the listing for that number. Is important to keep in mind when using the citators that they will track Lexis headnotes when you are in Shepard's, and Westlaw headnotes when you are in KeyCite. Using the headnote from *Gonzales v. Raich* highlighted in Chapter 3— Headnote 2 from Westlaw or Headnote 5 from Lexis, both concerning the power of Congress to regulate activities affecting interstate commerce—you are able to limit your citing cases to only those that discuss that particular point of law. To make this functionality even more powerful, you can combine it with the filtering functions discussed above: date, depth of treatment, jurisdiction etc.

It is worth noting that for some cases there are few or no citing references in Shepard's or KeyCite. In such situations a citator is of little help in a search for related cases. The fact that no citations can be found, however, may itself have some meaning. Several court decisions have mentioned the lack of citations as an indication that earlier decisions are of limited merit or scope.[7]

e.   Secondary Material and Annotations

In addition to the references to citing cases, Shepard's and KeyCite listings include citations indicating when a decision has been mentioned in secondary sources and annotations. These may include treatises, practice guides, legal encyclopedias, law reviews, or increasingly to briefs and other court filings. These are the kind of sources which can provide important context for you in your research. With some exceptions, these secondary sources will be different depending on the citator you are using. Unsurprisingly KeyCite will place you in the Westlaw universe of secondary materials, while Shepard's puts you in the Lexis world.

Treatises and practice guides are larger tomes covering a topic, e.g., Wigmore on Evidence or Bittker on the Regulation of Interstate and Foreign Commerce, which attempt to bring together what practitioners need to know. An article in a law review or bar journal also may provide useful background.

An underutilized resource that does appear in both systems is one of our favorites, *American Law Reports (ALR)*. Finding an

---

[7]   In *Meadow Brook National Bank v. Recite,* 302 F.Supp. 62, 82 (E.D. La. 1969), the federal district court in applying Louisiana law noted that an 1865 Louisiana Supreme Court case relied upon by the plaintiff was "clearly a maverick decision . . . totally ignored by every subsequent decision on the subject."

The courts in *Jeffres v. Countryside Homes of Lincoln, Inc.,* 333 N.W.2d 754, 764 (Neb. 1983), and *Amalgamated Casualty Insurance Co. v. Helms,* 212 A.2d 311, 319 (Md. 1965), used the absence of citations to denigrate decisions from other states which they did not care to follow.

ALR annotation which cites your case may open a door into an entirely new area of research. The ALR authors basically decide what's an interesting point of law and then write an exhaustive research memo on that topic. If your issues appears in multiple jurisdictions they tell you what's happening in every applicable jurisdiction. KeyCiting *Gonzales v. Raich* will turn up the ALR Annotation, *"Construction and Application of Controlled Substances Act, 21 U.S.C.A. §§ 801 et seq.—U.S. Supreme Court Cases"* 30 A.L.R. Fed. 2d 137. The ALR annotation "collects and discusses all U.S. Supreme Court cases that have considered the construction and application of the CSA." That is a lot of work that has been done for you. Take advantage of it. We believe that citators can be a crucial center of the research process.

f.   Further Features to Limit Results

Remember how we kept emphasizing that Shepard's and KeyCite would show you every mention of a case? Did you shudder to think of yourself wading through the 6,000+ citing references to *Gonzales v. Raich*? Using citators can plunge you into a never ending vortex of cases citing cases citing cases. You have the power to avoid that by using features within the systems that we have outlined—limiting citing cases by jurisdiction, date, headnote. We humbly suggest you learn to use such power judiciously. With lawyerly common sense you can reduce a list of a thousand cases to only those that have at least a paragraph of discussion about your case.

It gets even better. Both systems allow you to use terms and connectors to search the full-text of the cases that cited your case for words, facts or concepts that will bring you closer to those cases most related to yours. On both systems it is called "search within results" and appears as a search box when you are looking at your lists of citing references. This is powerful feature that you need to aware of.

Conclusion

Citators are a beautiful thing. Not only will they protect you from making a fool of yourself in front of a judge, they will put you on the trail of every decision that impacts your case. Just as importantly they allow you to expand out your research by finding relevant secondary sources that will more often than not be the best place to start and give context to your specific research issues. While you are a law student you will be able to play with both citators. Figure out which one is better at scratching your research itch.

Illustrations

CITATORS: KEYCITE HISTORY

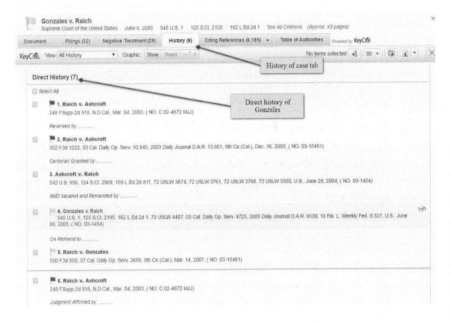

CITATORS: KEYCITE CITING REFERENCES

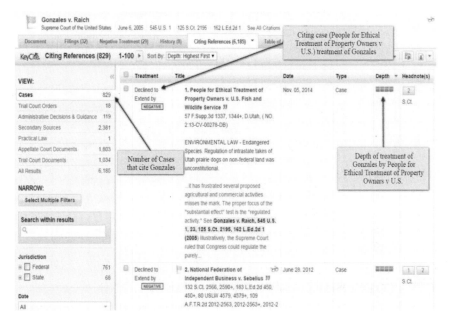

CITATORS: SHEPARD'S

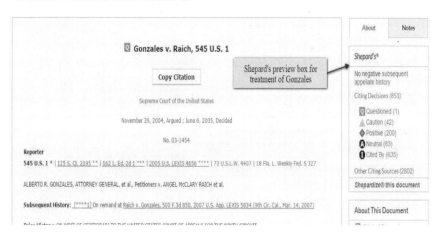

CITATORS: SHEPARD'S APPELLATE HISTORY

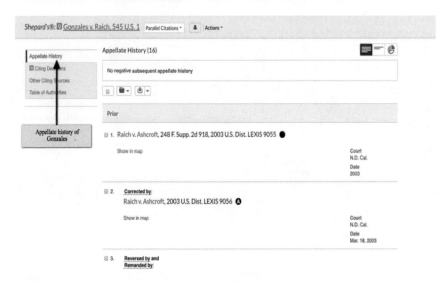

CITATORS: SHEPARD'S CITING DECISIONS

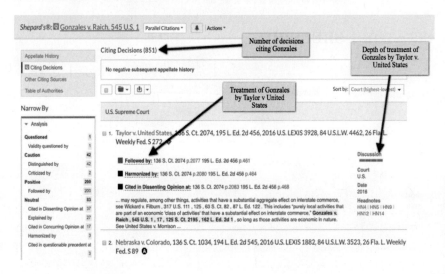

CHAPTER 5

STATUTES, SHORT AND SWEET

We debated leaving this chapter out, or tacking something about statutes onto the end of case finding and leaving it at that. But statutes are already given such short shrift by the first year of law school that we thought that denying them their own chapter would just be cruel and unusual. So here's the plan:

- We'll explain why we finally decided to talk at some length about statutes.

- We'll tell you in what forms they're published.

- We'll tell you a bit about how to find them

- Michael made a video about them that you can check.

I. WHY INCLUDE THIS CHAPTER?

During your first year of law school it will seem to you that lawyers spend all their time weighing one case against another, pondering which common law principle comes closest to solving the legal puzzle at hand. We decided we shouldn't leave you with the impression that we were trying to fool you too. Here's the truth: in practice, the majority of appellate decisions today involve the application or interpretation of statutes. When you venture into the real world it is much more likely that you will be researching a statute rather than a case. Statutes and other related legislative forms[1] constitute the second category of primary legal sources. Checking to see if there is a relevant statute should become one of your first instincts when approaching a legal research issue. If you do find a controlling statute in an annotated code, you've struck legal research gold.

This chapter will focus mostly on the general forms a statute takes and what research hooks will be found with them. All

---

[1] The term "legislation" can be broadly construed to include constitutions, statutes, treaties, municipal charters and ordinances, interstate compacts, and reorganization plans. We won't be troubling you with descriptions of all of them because, frankly, all you'll probably be dealing with in your first year is a state or a federal statute.

forms of statutes are reproduced online but, although this might shock you, it's still often easier to use the books.

Much like the situation of the court systems, the U.S. Congress and the legislature of each of the fifty states has its own structure and procedure for the initiation and passage of legislation. You shouldn't worry about learning the vocabulary and intricacies for all of the jurisdictions right now. Statutory publications, however, share some basic characteristics, and if you concentrate on the similarities we outline below, you can know what to expect in any jurisdiction.

II. THE PATTERN

Each of the jurisdictions in the United States issues its legislative publications according to a pattern. The names of the specific publications differ among the jurisdictions, but the generic equivalent always exists. The simplified pattern of statutory publication is as follows, and we've added the corresponding name of the publications for the federal system:

Session Law

United States Statutes at Large

Code

United States Code

Annotated Code

United States Code Annotated (USCA)
United States Code Service (USCS)

a.   Slip Laws

"Slip laws" are separately issued pamphlets, each of which contains the text of a single legislative act. They exist, but that may already be more than you need to know for our purposes. You won't see one as a first year law student. You won't even see one on the illustration above. In fact, it's unlikely that you'll ever see one in paper. However, when the federal government or one of the states posts new legislative acts online, it is generally in slip law form.

b.   Session Laws

The term "session laws" refers to the permanent publication, in chronological sequence, of the slip laws enacted during a legislative session. At the federal level, the volumes are called *Statutes at Large*. At each new legislative session the first law passed is named, "1", the second, "2," and the thirty-ninth, "39." Most states call these "chapters." Federal session laws are called "public laws." You'll almost never hear a state statute called, "chapter x," but it is quite common for the federal public law number to be used to identify a statute. *The Bluebook* or *ALWD Citation Manual* will help you decipher what is the proper citation for the papers you write, but the 425th law passed by the 110th U.S. Congress can be written:

P.L. 110–425

While session laws in paper form will have subject indexes and tables indicating which laws have been modified or repealed by the new legislation, they are not practical tools for most research.

c.   Statutory Compilations or Codes

A "code" is a publication of the public, general and permanent statutes of a jurisdiction in a fixed subject or topical arrangement. There is no perfect subject arrangement, some jurisdictions use lots of subject breakdowns, some use just a few. Each subject is usually referred to as a "title." The federal government uses fifty-three titles. It really does not matter how you cut the subject pie up as long as it works. Statutory codes preserve the original language of the session laws more or less intact, but rearrange and group them under broad subject categories. This ensures that all family law statutes, for example, end up together and in the right order.

Statutory codes may appear in either official or unofficial editions. Official statutory codes are published or sanctioned by the government, and it is usually this form of a statute to which you must cite. Codes normally include the text of the law and brief editorial notes as to the authority and historical development of the law. The official code for the laws of the federal government is called the *United States Code,* or *USC.* Your state may or may not have an official code.[2]

Despite their convenience in providing subject access, official codes have certain shortcomings. They are often issued very slowly, their editorial notes won't be adequate for most statutory research, and their indexes aren't usually very well done.

d.   Annotated Codes

Bob loves annotated codes. (Michael thinks they're pretty darn cool, too.) Annotated codes pull together information from all corners of the legal universe, especially cases and hook all this information up to the statutory sections. Frequently when you read a statute you will not know what it means until you read the cases that interpret it. Legislatures sometimes do this on purpose. To facilitate the passage of a law, ambiguous language is used and it is up to the courts to parse out the meaning. The annotated code takes you by the hand and leads you to relevant cases and other great stuff, too.

An annotated code reproduces the text and subject arrangement of the official code. It also incorporates new legislation, revisions and amendments, and deletes repealed laws. In paper form they are updated and supplemented more frequently than their official counterparts by means of pocket parts and pamphlet supplements.[3] Their unique editorial

---

[2] California, for example, doesn't have an official code. Instead, it has two unofficial codes.

[3] Pocket parts are paper updates stuck into the back of each volume. Pamphlets are issued when the pocket part becomes so thick it no longer fits into the back of the book. They're updated this way because it's too expensive to issue a new bound volume every year.

contribution to legal research is the inclusion of *annotations* after each statutory section. These include references to relevant judicial or administrative decisions, administrative code sections, encyclopedias, attorney general opinions, legislative history materials, law reviews, and treatises. Additionally, they have good indexing, using words and phrases that are in common use instead of legal jargon to help you find what you seek.

In the federal system, there are two annotated codes you need to know about, *United States Code Service,* published by Lexis, and *United States Code Annotated,* published by West. They are almost always referred to and written as *USCS* and *USCA,* respectively. Descriptions of the specific features found in these two publications, and of the *USC,* can be found in more comprehensive legal research texts.

A word of warning for you, though: the materials added by the editor *aren't the law,* so don't quote them in a paper or before a judge. They're only there to help you understand the law.

III. ELECTRONIC SOURCES, OF COURSE

Both Westlaw and Lexis reproduce annotated state and federal codes online. The online code databases are generally up to date within a few months or less; the session law databases are often up to date within weeks or days. The currency of these databases is indicated on scope or information screens, and should be checked before relying on an online search for current information.

The Westlaw and Lexis code databases are often most useful in situations where an issue is not adequately covered in indexes or where a combination of particular terms is important. The general scoop is, however, that if you're just starting your research, annotated codes are still easier to use as books. Why? Because statutory language is difficult (wait until you start reading them), and this makes them very hard to search using terms and connectors or even natural language searches. If you include annotations in your search you can end up flooded with false hits. Annotated codes, with their user-friendly indexing are just easier to manipulate in paper form. We know it's hard to believe (or accept), but it's still the truth.

Many states now park the text of their codes on a state-maintained website. Check out what the situation is in your state. The coverage will vary but some of them are quite good. Without the annotations though, the utility of such sites is limited.

At the end of this chapter we include examples of two statutes that are cited in *Gonzales v. Raich*. One is the beginning of the codification of the federal *Controlled Substances Act*, the other presents the beginning of the *California Compassionate Use Act*. These are screenshots from Lexis and Westlaw made at the end of 2016. If you looked them up when you are reading these words, they might look different but you will get the picture of the available resources.

IV.   THE PRACTICAL ADVICE

a.   Finding Statutes

Looking for statutes in a code is a very straightforward process. Start by breaking your issue down to relevant terms and catchphrases. Try looking them up in the index to the code for your jurisdiction. The index is likely to supply you with a citation to the relevant code section, or will give you a cross reference to try in the index. Now that doesn't sound too hard, does it?

If you already have a citation to the statute, you can, of course, skip the index and pull the section directly. Often, however, you don't have a citation, but you have what is called a "popular name." For an older statute, "popular name" usually means a name with which it has come to be associated with it over time, such as "The Securities Act of 1933." Most modern statutes, on the other hand, specify short titles by which they may be cited. These names, such as "Marine Plastic Pollution Research and Control Act of 1987," are also listed in popular name tables. (By now you have figured out that the word "popular" is used loosely. We are not talking Scarlett Johansson popular, we are talking about "the fact that a court once mentioned it" popular.) A Popular Name Table is generally found in the last index volume belonging to a code. This table is made up of alphabetical lists of statutes, providing citations to their session law and codified locations. Lexis and Westlaw have versions of their popular name tables online.

There will be other tables included with each code set such as tables that will cross reference you to a code section if all you have is a session law number. All we ask of you here is that you realize just how much information is packed into these tools. You will be sent to cases, commentaries, practice books, administrative rules and more, all of them relevant to your statute.

b.   Updating Statutes

Just as finding decisions is not all there is to case research, finding statutes through indexes, tables, or other means is just the first step of statutory research. You will have to verify that a statute is still in force and figure out how it has been affected by subsequent legislation and by judicial decision.

The primary method for updating the statutes is the annotated code. Annotated codes provide regularly updated information on the validity and treatment of legislation. The paper version of the code will be kept current by the pocket parts or pamphlets we mentioned above. A common research mistake is to use only the pocket part and to stop. Specific state research guides can be consulted when you are confronted with a particular legal research problem, and you can always check with a librarian to find all the components necessary to update your code section. Generally speaking, you'll need to check the pocket parts and the advance session law publications (which are issued during the current legislative session) as well.

While we have discouraged you from trying to find statutes on Lexis or Westlaw, we are happy to point out that updating statutes using the online systems is quite easy. If using Lexis or Westlaw, be certain of the coverage of the database. How recently has new information been added? Is there new or pending legislation that should be checked? Both Lexis and Westlaw will indicate the currentness of the code section you are researching. They will also indicate through the flags that you have already seen in KeyCite and Shepards whether there are cases or pending legislation that may affect your particular code section.

We keep saying this, but it bears repeating: take the training in how to use Lexis and Westlaw and look for the handouts and training materials that the companies make available online. While the research systems are trying to win your love, take advantage.

c.   Context

When using annotated codes, be sure that you understand the context of the section that you are reading. Legislatures, especially Congress, pass gigantic laws with multiple parts. A part of a new law may be placed into one of the titles of a code. It may have its own definitions and even statements of intent. Dipping into a code for a single section, or part of a section, can mislead you. Step back and take stock of where your section fits into the larger structure. Doing so can save you from heading down the wrong road. Context is king.

Have We Forgotten Something?

We considered explaining how to use administrative materials. Using administrative rules and regulations and the decisions of administrative boards and panels is central to much real life research. But you are very unlikely to run into any administrative materials in your first semester. We wanted to keep this book as relevant to your life as possible, so we decided to let it go. But in case you are interested, Michael has made a video that will show you the basics.

SUMMARY

Though you may do only a bit of statutory research during your first year of law school, you should understand what statutes are and how to find them. Annotated codes are powerful research tools. Give them a try. Here are two screenshots of statutes cited in *Gonzales v. Raich.*

Illustrations

A Printout of a Statute from WestLaw

21 U.S.C.A. § 841

Citation to
annotated code

§ 841. Prohibited acts A

Effective: August 3, 2010

Currentness

Text of the law
begins here

(a) Unlawful acts

Except as authorized by this subchapter, it shall be unlawful for any person knowingly or intentionally--

(1) to manufacture, distribute, or dispense, or possess with intent to manufacture, distribute, or dispense, a controlled substance; or

(2) to create, distribute, or dispense, or possess with intent to distribute or dispense, a counterfeit substance.

(b) Penalties

Except as otherwise provided in section 849, 859, 860, or 861 of this title, any person who violates subsection (a) of this section shall be sentenced as follows:

(1)(A) In the case of a violation of subsection (a) of this section involving—

[...]

Text of the law ends here.
Remember: nothing except the text is citable.

Credits list in chronological order citations to session laws that have enacted, amended, or renumbered the section.

CREDIT(S)

(Pub.L. 91-513, Title II, § 401, Oct. 27, 1970, 84 Stat. 1260; Pub.L. 95-633, Title II, § 201, Nov. 10, 1978, 92 Stat. 3774; Pub.L. 96-359, § 8(c), Sept. 26, 1980, 94 Stat. 1194; Pub.L. 98-473, Title II, §§ 224(a), 502, 503(b)(1), (2), Oct. 12, 1984, 98 Stat. 2030, 2068, 2070; Pub.L. 99-570, Title I, §§ 1002, 1003(a), 1004(a), 1005(a), 1103, Title XV, § 15005, Oct. 27, 1986, 100 Stat. 3207-2, 3207-5, 3207-6, 3207-11, 3207-192; Pub.L. 100-690, Title VI, §§ 6055, 6254(h), 6452(a), 6470(g), (h), 6479, Nov. 18, 1988, 102 Stat. 4318, 4367, 4371, 4378, 4381; Pub.L. 101-647, Title X, § 1002(e), Title XII, § 1202, Title XXXV, § 3599K, Nov. 29, 1990, 104 Stat. 4828, 4830, 4932; Pub.L. 103-322, Title IX, § 90105(a), (c), Title XVIII, § 180201(b)(2)(A), Sept. 13, 1994, 108 Stat. 1987, 1988, 2047; Pub.L. 104-237, Title II, § 206(a), Title III, § 302(a), Oct. 3, 1996, 110 Stat. 3103, 3105; Pub.L. 104-305, § 2(a), (b)(1), Oct. 13, 1996, 110 Stat. 3807; Pub.L. 105-277, Div. E, § 2(a), Oct. 21, 1998, 112 Stat. 2681-759; Pub.L. 106-172, §§ 3(b)(1), 5(b), 9, Feb. 18, 2000, 114 Stat. 9, 10, 13; Pub.L. 107-273, Div. B, Title III, § 3005(a), Title IV, § 4002(d)(2)(A), Nov. 2, 2002, 116 Stat. 1805, 1809; Pub.L. 109-177, Title VII, §§ 711(f)(1)(B), 732, Mar. 9, 2006, 120 Stat. 262, 270; Pub.L. 109-248, Title II, § 201, July 27, 2006, 120 Stat. 611; Pub.L. 110-425, § 3(e), (f), Oct. 15, 2008, 122 Stat. 4828, 4829; Pub.L. 111-220, §§ 2(a), 4(a), Aug. 3, 2010, 124 Stat. 2372.)

Notes of Decisions (7676)

Footnotes

Notes of Decisions are summaries of cases that have interpreted the particular statute in question. This feature shows you how the statute has been applied by courts. This particular statute has been cited in cases 7,676 times.

[1] So in original. Probably should be "health".

[2] So in original. Probably should be "section".

21 U.S.C.A. § 841, 21 USCA § 841
Current through P.L. 114-244.

Cal Health & Saf Code § 11362.5

Cal Health & Saf Code § 11362.5

Citation to annotated code

Currency Statement Missing

Deering's California Code Annotated > *HEALTH AND SAFETY CODE* > *Division 10, Uniform Controlled Substances Act* > *Chapter 6. Offenses and Penalties* > *Article 2, Marijuana*

Text of the law begins here

§ 11362.5. Use of marijuana for medical purposes

(a) This section shall be known and may be cited as the Compassionate Use Act of 1996.

(b)

   (1) The people of the State of California hereby find and declare that the purposes of the Compassionate Use Act of 1996 are as follows:

      (A) To ensure that seriously ill Californians have the right to obtain and use marijuana for medical purposes where that medical use is deemed appropriate and has been recommended by a physician who has determined that the person's *health* would benefit from the use of marijuana in the treatment of cancer, anorexia, AIDS, chronic pain, spasticity, glaucoma, arthritis, migraine, or any other illness for which marijuana provides relief.

      (B) To ensure that patients and their primary caregivers who obtain and use marijuana for medical purposes upon the recommendation of a physician are not subject to criminal prosecution or sanction.

      (C) To encourage the federal and state governments to implement a plan to provide for the safe and affordable distribution of marijuana to all patients in medical need of marijuana.

   (2) Nothing in this section shall be construed to supersede legislation prohibiting persons from engaging in conduct that endangers others, nor to condone the diversion of marijuana for nonmedical purposes.

(c) Notwithstanding any other provision of law, no physician in this state shall be punished, or denied any right or privilege, for having recommended marijuana to a patient for medical purposes.

(d) Section 11357, relating to the possession of marijuana, and Section 11358, relating to the cultivation of marijuana, shall not apply to a patient, or to a patient's primary caregiver, who possesses or cultivates marijuana for the personal medical purposes of the patient upon the written or oral recommendation or approval of a physician.

(e) For the purposes of this section, "primary caregiver" means the individual designated by the person exempted under this section who has consistently assumed responsibility for the housing, *health*, or safety of that person.

Text of the law ends here.
Remember: nothing except the text is citable.

Cal Health & Saf Code § 11362.5

> Provides background on how
> the statute was enacted.

History

Adopted by the voters, Prop. 215 § 1, effective November 6, 1996.

Annotations

> The annotations section includes four main subgroups: notes, case notes, opinion
> notes, and research references and practice aids. Notes may explain certain sections
> of the statute not covered in the main text. Case notes are summaries of cases that
> have interpreted the particular statute in question. This feature shows you how the
> statute has been applied by courts. Opinion notes references opinions written by
> other judges, lawyers, or legal authorities regarding the statute. Research references
> and practical aids contain any references to the statute in law review articles or other
> written applications.

Notes

Note

Proposition 215 (1996) provides:

SECTION. 2. If any provision of this measure or the application thereof to any person or circumstance is held
invalid, that invalidity shall not affect other provisions or applications of the measure that can be given effect without
the invalid provision or application, and to this end the provisions of his measure are severable.

Case Notes

1. Generally

2. Constitutionality

3. Construction

3.5. Construction with Other Law

4. Particular Applications

5. Burden of Proof

6. Return of Seized Marijuana

7. Relationship to Federal Laws

Cal Health & Saf Code § 11362.5

8. Probation

9. Evidence

10. Local Regulation

Opinion Notes

Attorney General's Opinions:

The statewide registry and identification card program for medical marijuana users preempts the operation of a city's own registry and identification card program, but a city may adopt and enforce other ordinances consistent with the statewide program. *88 Cal. Ops. Atty. Gen. 113.*

Research References & Practice Aids

Cross References:

Medical Marijuana Program: H & S C §§ 11362.7 et seq.

Collateral References:

Cal. Forms Pleading & Practice (Matthew Bender(R)) ch 214 "Drugs And Pharmacists".

Cal. Points & Authorities (Matthew Bender(R)) ch 81 "Discovery: Privileges And Other Discovery Limitations," § 81.251.

Cal Criminal Defense Practice (Matthew Bender(R)) ch 145 "Narcotics and Alcohol Offenses" § 145.01(3).

Cal. Employment Law (Matthew Bender(R)), § 60.04.

Judicial Council of California Criminal Jury Instructions (LexisNexis Matthew Bender), CALCRIM No. 2350, Sale, Furnishing, etc., of Marijuana.

Judicial Council of California Criminal Jury Instructions (LexisNexis Matthew Bender), CALCRIM No. 2351, Offering to Sell, Furnish, etc., Marijuana.

[...]

Law Review Articles:

Good Cop, Bad Cop: Federal Prosecution of State-Legalized Medical Marijuana Use After United States v. Lopez. *88 Cal LR 1575.*

The Growing Debate on Medical Marijuana: Federal Power vs. States Rights. 37 Cal Western LR 369.

Proposition 215: legal strategies for the medicinal use of marijuana. *21 LA Law, No. 5, p. 21.*

[...]

Annotations:

Propriety of Requirement, as Condition of Probation, That Defendant Refrain from Use of Intoxicants. *46 ALR6th 241.*

Cal Health & Saf Code § 11362.5

Construction and Application of Medical Marijuana Laws and Medical Necessity Defense to Marijuana Laws. _50 ALR6th 353_

Propriety of Employer's Discharge of or Failure to Hire Employee Due to Employee's Use of Medical Marijuana. _57 ALR6th 285_

Preemption of State Regulation of Controlled Substances by Federal Controlled Substances Act. _60 ALR6th 175_

Hierarchy Notes:

Div. 10 Note

Div. 10, Ch. 6 Note

Div. 10, Ch. 6, Art. 2 Note

End of Document

Final Takeaways

1. Training

Be sure to take the trainings offered by the information providers. It is important that you get trained on more than one system and don't just go with the research system that gave you the best colored post-it notes.

2. Print Resources

Don't shy away from using resources in paper. We mentioned that annotated codes can oftentimes be easier to navigate in their analog form. Have more than electronic research skills in your research portfolio.

3. Law Librarians

Make sure you ask your friendly law librarian questions when you hit a legal research road block. Law librarians want to help you. They are on your side. You would be foolish not to take advantage of these human resources.

4. Free Resources

Take the time to become familiar with resources offered for free by courts, government agencies, universities and non-profits. Clients are less willing to pay for research services than in the past so knowing the reliable and trustworthy sites where you can find cases, statutes and regulations is becoming more important.

5.   Research Strategy

We wanted to give you some general trips on research strategy so we made a video about it. Check it out.